KT-423-669

'*Bid farewell to Scotland, and cross to Fife.*' This historic proverb seems to encapsulate the relative isolation of the Kingdom from the rest of Scotland, largely the consequence of its physical restraints. This firth- and sea-girt peninsula, with its land-neck guarded by hills, forests and bogs, certainly discouraged indiscriminate pillagers and colonisers. The Romans seem to have avoided Fife, coastal raids by the Danes and the Norsemen were sporadic, and punitive strikes by the English (despite unforgivable damage by Cromwell's men to some of the buildings) were rare. The Kingdom was therefore spared many of the ravages endured by the rest of Central Scotland, and thus was perhaps more able to retain its concentrated essence of Scottish architecture.

The '*folk of Fife*' (in Sir Walter Scott's terminology) inherited a strong sense of identity, possibly indeed from the time when it was a regional kingdom of the Pictish confederation. That sense of identity bred a fierce spirit of independence which ensured that Fife, alone of all the counties in Scotland, kept its ancient boundaries discrete and intact as a region, when all the others were re-organised and amalgamated into the massive and flavourless fiefdoms that they are today.

Yet the Firths of Forth and Tay were hardly just barriers, waiting to be bridged in the 19th and 20th centuries. They were busy waterways, crossed by kings and bishops, pilgrims and merchants. For the principal route north and east to Arbroath, Aberdeen, Banff and Moray began with a crossing from Edinburgh to Burntisland, and around the coast of St Andrews and thence north to Tayport. Many stayed, for Fife was, as it remains, a place to go to rather than to pass through. It was a cockpit of Scots history. St Andrews, one of its greatest towns, and oldest university, occupied its chilly North Sea clifftop. For centuries its primates were amongst Scotland's most powerful statesmen. Royal palaces of immense splendour were constructed at Falkland and at Dunfermline, and developed in importance during the unfolding history of the six Jacobean kings. Fife's early membership of a European and Nordic Economic Community was recognised by the kings, with 15 out its 18 Royal Burghs being ports – many founded by James VI specifically to encourage Baltic trade. From these thriving ports dotted along its 115 mile coastline, ships plied back and forth to France, to the Baltic

The Doocot at Letham Lands

Opposite:
Gateway to Fife – The Forth Bridge photographed in its Centenary Year by Colin Wishart

3

Measured drawing of St Rule's, St Andrews, (see page 118) by J Russell Walker

RIAS Library

towns and to the Low Countries. Far from being isolated or parochial, Fife was thereby freely exposed to international influences.

Nor was the Kingdom immune to national change. Once the Reformation brought an end to the pervasive power of the established religious order in 1560, and the royal influence with its attendant patronage faded once the court moved to London in 1603, some of Fife's finest buildings went into irreversible decline. As new lands were discovered, merchant ships had new oceans to sail, and the economic supremacy of Scotland moved to the west at the expense of Fife.

The agricultural revolution at the end of the 18th century was beneficial to Fife, with revived exports of grain and potatoes, and the flourishing of brewing and distilling. Home-weaving, practised in the Kingdom since the 15th century, was replaced by the powerloom in the mid 19th century and vastly expanded, particularly in Dunfermline. By the late 19th century also, the coal industry – whose roots dated back to the 13th century – burgeoned, and began to dominate and overwhelm central Fife. The change from rural to industrial is reflected in the fact that the population employed on land shrunk from 31% in 1801 to 4.5% 100 years later. Despite the overwhelming impression that remains even today of rolling hills and rich farmland, the Kingdom had become fundamentally urbanised.

Now that its traditional industries have declined, Fife generates electrical power, processes natural gas, and has nurtured many new enterprises, particularly in electronics. Inevitably, the history of these changes are recorded in the richness and the variety of the architecture of the Kingdom.

Organisation of the Guide

This Guide is an illustrated architectural guide to the history and character of the Kingdom of Fife, as interpreted through its architecture. It is divided into 8 sections (see plan below) traversed in broad outline as follows: **Dunfermline and District** – North Queensferry to Dunfermline – north and west to Kincardine – east along coast to Aberdour; **Kirkcaldy and Coast** – Burntisland, east to Kirkcaldy and on to Leven; **Leven and Ore Valleys** – up Ore valley to Cowdenbeath, and up Leven valley to Leslie; **Eden Valley (south)** – Falkland to Dairsie Bridge, including valleys of Craigrothie and Ceres Burns; **Eden Valley (north)** – Gateside

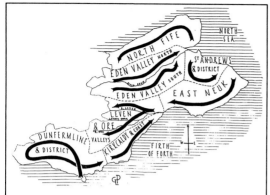

to Guardbridge; **St Andrews**; **East Neuk** –
Kingsbarns, round the coast to Lundin Links;
and ending with **North Fife** – Tayport to
Newburgh including the valley of Motray Water.

Text arrangement

Entries for principal buildings follow the
sequence of name (or number), address, date and
architect (if known). Lesser buildings are
contained within paragraphs. Both demolished
buildings and unrealised projects are included if
appropriate. In general, the dates given are
those of the design (if known) or of the beginning
of construction (if not). Text in the small column
is illustrative of less architectural aspects of the
story of the Kingdom of Fife.

Map references

The numbers do not refer to page numbers but
to numbers in the text itself. Where buildings
are concentrated, space has allowed only a few
numbers sufficient for visitors to take bearings.
Numbers in the Index refer to pages.

Author's acknowledgements

To Charles McKean for his Procrustean efforts
over three years to reduce a discursive draft to
the taut format of the series; Colin Wishart, for
his help, encouragement and photographs which
say much more than my words; Dorothy Smith
and Lena Smith, for their invaluable secretarial
assistance; Betty, my wife, companion and co-
driver on all my surveys.

Other acknowledgements

Colin Wishart would like to thank all those who
assisted in the compilation of illustrations: the
RCAHMS, RIAS Library, National Gallery,

RIAS Library

*Measured drawing by J Russell
Walker, of St Salvator's Collegiate
Church, St Andrews (see page 122)*

Bourne Fine Art, Andrew Neil of Arts in Fife for splendid prints and photographs, Father Michael Carey, Ian Forrest; and particularly my friend Malcolm Thomson of Studio-M, Dundee, for excellent and unstinting photographic services. The RIAS wishes to record its gratitude to David Cowling for steadfast support, to Ron Tremmell and to David Walker.

Access to properties
Many of the buildings described in this guide are open to the public, or are visible from a public road or footpath. Some are private, and readers are requested to respect the occupiers' privacy.

Sponsors
It would have been impossible to publish this volume at its low sale price without the generous support and financial assistance of sponsors: notably the Fife Regional Council, the Landmark Trust, Kirkcaldy and Dunfermline District Councils and the Glenrothes Development Corporation.

'Iona of the East' – Inchcolm in the Firth of Forth photographed by Colin Wishart

Dunfermline and District

FORTH BRIDGES

This natural narrow on the Forth, the historic southern gateway to Fife where the ferry plied for almost 1000 years has become a showcase for engineering skill.

Forth Bridge, 1883-90, J Fowler & B Baker
Its distinctive silhouette of three gigantic double cantilevers overshadows relatively delicate detail. **Forth Road Bridge**, 1958-64, Freeman Fox & Partners with G Gilbert Scott & Partners. Belies, in the simple curves of its suspension, the immense 156m height of its slender towers and 2.5km length of cambered span.

NORTH QUEENSFERRY

Below the thunder of the trains and the roar of traffic (this is still the main route into Fife, albeit 45m above the Forth) the community of North Queenferry, now beached by history, tries hard to come to terms with a minor role. Stage props from the past remain. The **Town Pier**, 1810-18, J Rennie (extended for steamships J Telfer in 1828) and **Railway Pier**, 1877 (last used by car ferry, 1964), are both seaweed-covered and derelict. At the Pierhead is **Signal Tower**, c.1810, a squat hexagonal with copper domed lantern and **Tower (Hooley) House**, c.1810, former HQ of the ferry, now private dwelling – a crenellated, buttressed octagonal with an unfortunate addition, c.1875. On the site of the 18th-century coaching inn, Hope Tavern, Main Street, stands the cubic mass of the **Albert Hotel**, c.1850, with pilastered entrance flanked by Edwardian bow windows.

St James' Chapel, Chapel Place, 14th/15th century
Little more than a west gable with mullioned window. Some 18th-century houses have been carefully modernised, e.g. **No 2 Post Office Lane** with forestair, and **No 10**, 1776; along Main Street **Brae House**, 1771, and **White House**, 1778, with three-faced sundial.

Before their long haul up The Brae, coachhorses were watered at the **Waterloo Well**, an artisan curved gable and carved ship (dated 1816) in commemoration of the battle. On the west side of The Brae, a pair of pantiled **houses**, c.1770, features forestairs, straight and curved. Near the sharp bend is the **Old School House**, 1827.

Wishart

Signal Tower

David I, in 1129 granted Dunfermline Abbey the rights of the ferry. In 1590 ownership passed to proprietors of neighbouring lands. Early in the 18th century Defoe *'crossed the river at Queensferry, seven miles west of Edinburgh into the shire of Fife'*. In 1765, Thomas Gray crossed *'in a four-oared yawl without a sail'*. By the end of the 18th century the pressure of passengers, goods and mail resulted in much-needed road improvements. The Ferry was 'nationalised' in 1809 and investment made in ships and harbour facilities. The railway ferry to Burntisland reduced the traffic in the mid 19th century but the 20th-century advent of the motorist increased the demand (resulting in the construction of four ferry boats from 1934 to 1956) which lasted until the Road Bridge was opened in September 1964.

Top *Rosyth Castle by Francis Grose, c.1787*. Above *Pitreavie prior to its additions*

Dunfermline from the Abbey porch by Joseph Swan c.1834

1 Rosyth Castle, late 15th-century
Once on an island in the Forth, this large, plain tower is now enveloped by Rosyth Dockyard. Built by Sir James Stewart, it was extended into a courtyard in the 17th century when the tower's two large mullioned and transomed windows, which merely emphasise its original stark appearance, were added. Of the 16th/17th-century barmkin, only the gateway and armorial panels above (one dated 1561) are now of any significance. The early 16th-century **Doocot** is unusual with barrel-vault and gable roof over.

2 Pitreavie, *c.*1630
The original four-storey house had almost classical symmetry, taking the peculiarly Scots U-plan, with projecting wings, and turreted turnpike stairs in the re-entrants. As part of a Baronial flourish in 1885, Charles Kinnear thickened the main block, advanced the south gables of the wings, and provided canted bay windows. HQ of Commander Northern Maritime Air Region Security; access is difficult.

DUNFERMLINE

The favoured seat of Scots kings over three centuries lines a 80m-high ridge 5km inland from the Forth. The town's origins lie in the small burgh of Regality which belonged to the richly endowed Benedictine Abbey of the Holy Trinity and St Margaret. It was a centre of medieval pilgrimage, and the supposed burial place of Robert the Bruce. The King usually stayed in the Abbey's guest house, which James IV converted into a palace in 1540. The town became a Royal Burgh in 1588 but the departure

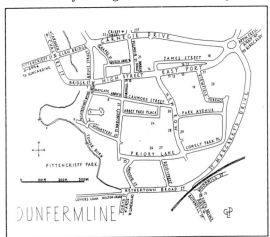

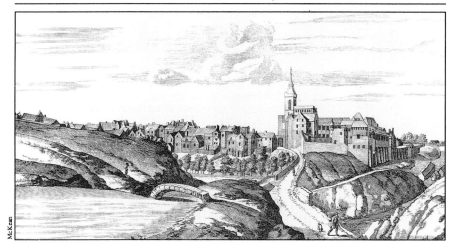

Dunfermline in the late 17th century, by Captain John Slezer. Note the great Renaissance palace with its circular stairtower on the site of the western cloister

of the Court for England in 1603 spelt the end for Dunfermline as a Royal seat, and there was little else – a village of perhaps 100 souls. What there was – and the Abbot's house in Maygate may be a sole survivor – was burnt in a great fire in 1624.

The local manufacture of linen began early (the conduct of the 'wabsters' features in the Magistrates' Records of 1491) and by the 18th century its damask table linen acquired a national reputation. In the mid 19th century the industry flourished although power-looms made the handweavers redundant.

It declined irrevocably after the First World War. As the 20th century got under way, the surrounding coalfields (some of which dated from the 13th century) were abandoned. They have been replaced as a principal employer by Rosyth Dockyard, which expanded from 1909, until its current slimming down and diversification. Improved communications have encouraged the growth of new industrial estates, and of Dunfermline's role as a dormitory for Edinburgh.

3 **Dunfermline Abbey**, from 1128
The finest surviving example of Scots Norman architecture. The great monastic church, the nave of which is a simplified version of that at Durham, was set on the highest part of a bluff on the east side of the Tower Burn, incidentally superimposed upon the remains of Queen Margaret's Church, 1072. Nave and aisle now act as a form of vestibule to the 19th-century church. Apprehension about the stability of the

Sir Patrick Geddes' plan for Dunfermline (*above*). The publication, in 1904, of his Report – *City Development: a Study of Parks, Gardens and Culture Institutes* established Patrick Geddes, a botanist by profession, as a town planner of the first rank. It demonstrated to the world at large, how existing resources, physical, human and historical could, with realism and imagination, become the elements of urban renewal and development. Unfortunately, the bold spirit which inspired the Carnegie Trustees to give Geddes his first commission as town planner failed when it came to implementation.

Parish Church

walls resulted in the construction of its characteristic multi-staged flying buttresses in 1620-5. The tall, narrow west front lost the finely balanced composition of the 12th century with each addition. In 1400, the gable was refronted, and the north-west tower enlarged; in 1500, its parapet spire was added. The uncompleted 1811 rebuilding of the south-west tower by William Stark is diffident by comparison. The centrepiece is the magnificent, deeply recessed Romanesque doorway; and there is another fine example, faced by a 15th-century vaulted deep porch, on the north façade. The nave is timber roofed, the aisles are vaulted. Bold chevron and spiral carving on the massive round piers lightens the stony medieval gloom.

4 **Parish Church**, 1818-21, William Burn
Soaring, traceried Gothic shell on the site of the Abbey choir. It offers a bright, plaster-vaulted interior splashed by the colours of armorial standards.

5 **Pends,** 14th/15th century
The gatehouse ('pends') to the Abbey precinct links the cloister buildings on the east to the Guest House and Palace on the west side of the pedestrianised **Monastery Street.** The traffic now removed, the splendid masonry cliff can be studied in peace, the imagination given free rein. Note, above the two lancet-windowed undercroft storeys, the windows of the Refectory itself, and the magnificent cusped arch supporting the projection of the pulpitum (the place from which readings were given during mealtimes). The gables of the vaulted undercrofts of dorter and reredorter to the east reveal lancet windows which probably survived King Edward I's destruction of the Abbey in 1304. Note also the projecting passage at the west end which links the mid storey of the Refectory with the gatehouse. The tracery of the great 15th-century west window of the Refectory is exceptionally fine.

One interesting mural monument, 1602, in primitive classical style commemorates **William Shaw**, described, in Latin, as King's Master of Works, Master of Ceremonies and Chamberlain to the Queen. It goes on to state that Queen Anne ordered the monument to be set up to *'the memory of a most admirable and most upright man'.*

Of Dunfermline Abbey Edward I said *'not a church but a den of thieves ... a thorn in the eye of the English nation.'* Not surprisingly he ordered its destruction in 1304.

6 **Guest House**, 14th century
The Abbot's Guest House was converted to a palace *c.*1540 by King James IV, and again worked on in 1598-1600 for Queen Anne. The dramatic effect of its south façade, over 60m long by 18m high, can best be appreciated from **Pittencrieff Glen**, as an extension of the cliff face, complete with the arched buttresses of the kitchen undercroft. The skeleton of the palatial

Top *Dunfermline Abbey viewed from Pittencrieff Park.* Top right *The West Door* Centre right *17th-century flying buttresses reinforce the Nave.* Below right *Dunfermline from the south c.1834.* Above *Nave of the Abbey c.1846*

Abbot's House

The Coach for Edinburgh and the 'Fly' for Aberdour Ferry started in the shadow of the Abbey at the Old Inn, said to be the oldest in Dunfermline.

interior, with its wide mullioned windows, elaborate vaulting and the obvious historic alterations, is best surveyed from the roadway.

Old Inn, Kirkgate
Victorian reconstruction of an 18th-century coaching inn, now rendered in the conventional hostelry colours of white with black edging.

7 **City Chambers**, 1876-9, J C Walker
An elaborate French Gothic concoction with Scottish overtones, its Fettes-type clock steeple surges up from its narrow corner site to celebrate the mercantile prosperity of 19th-century weaving. **2-18 Maygate**, designed in 1896 by T Hyslop-Ure, is said to have been designed to complement the City Chambers, but the result is relatively restrained with red stone dressings and modest shell-headed doorways.

8 **Abbot's House**, 21 Maygate, from 16th century
Remains of a substantial town house with two projecting stair towers and corbelled turret stairs in the re-entrants. 17th-century extensions included entrance in north stair tower with lintel inscribed:
*'Sen Vord is thrall and thoct is fre
Keip veill thy tonge I coinsell the'*

Near the west gable is the **Market Cross**: the shaft is dated 1695.

Pittencrieff House enjoys a splendid parkland setting

Pittencrieff Park
Bought by Andrew Carnegie in 1902 and presented to the citizens of Dunfermline, a

Wishart

Andrew Carnegie (1837-1910) was born at 2 Moodie Street, son of a hand-loom weaver. In the Hungry Forties (1848) the family emigrated to America where he started work as a cotton worker. In 1901 when he retired from the Carnegie Steel Company which he had created he was a multi-millionaire. Some of the fruits of his astonishingly successful business career were bestowed on his native town *'to bring into the monstrous lives of the toiling masses of Dunfermline more sweetness and light.'* Among his many gifts are included Public Baths, 1877, Library 1881, Public Baths and Gymnasium, 1903, Pittencrieff Park, 1903, a School of Music, College of Hygiene and Physical Education and a number of Trusts.

munificence commemorated by his bronze **statue** by Richard Goulden, 1914. It stands near the **Louise Carnegie Memorial Gates**, 1928, a fine wrought-ironwork design by James Arnott set in Renaissance-style masonwork.

9 **Pittencrieff House**, *c*.1635, originally a plain rectangle plus a square stair tower (with moulded entrance doorway), centred on the south front. In 1731, dated on the skewputt, its dignity was enhanced with an extra floor. It was reconstructed with pleasant interiors by Sir Robert Lorimer, 1908-11, as a museum of local life. *Open to the Public; leaflet available*

Teahouse, 1927, by John Fraser and **Music Pavilion**, 1936, by F A MacDonald & Partners are variations of Cape Dutch. Timber framework is painted black; roof pitches are low and eaves are wide; there is distinctive curved glass at wallhead level.

The statistics of Dunfermline linen trade read: 1749, 400 hand-looms; 1788, 900; 1792, 1200; 1821, 1800; 1845, 3000 (mostly male operatives). Power-looms were introduced in the mid 19th century and by 1905 there were 5265 power-looms operated mostly by women.

Above left *Stimulating variety in the Teahouse and Music Pavilion.* Below *Civic aspirations revealed by Guildhall, left, and City Chambers at foot of High Street*

10 **Guildhall**, 79 High Street, 1805, Archibald Elliot
An imposing classical composition, despite alteration, and filleted interior. A three-storey block, with a two-storey advanced, pedimented centre, sits on a rock-faced basement. Its well-proportioned steeple, added in 1811, manages its geometric transformation from square to cylinder with ease and soars disdainfully above the commercialised jumble which surrounds it.

High Street
Along the ridge, High Street and East Port exhibit the irregularity of their medieval origin; their façades now much damaged by vulgar fascias. It is the exceptions which catch the eye:
11 **15 East Port** (Prudential Assurance Office, now District Finance Department), 1914-16, Paul Waterhouse, is Greek neoclassic, perhaps

Wishart

Robert Henryson, (*c.*1420-90), a schoolmaster of Dunfermline and one of the makars, the Scottish poets mourned along with Chaucer himself by William Dunbar in his *Lament for the Makars*, 1508:
'In Dunfermline he has done roune
With Maister Robert Henryson
Sir John the Ross embraced has he;
Timor Mortis conturbat me.'

Daniel Defoe found a town *in its full perfection of decay ... the people hereabout are poor, but would be much poorer if they had not the manufacture of linnen for their support.* In the early 19th century it expanded with the same prosperity common to most Scottish towns which were centres of manufacture. In 1843, it had *a fine appearance, and, with its splendid church and spires, forms a most imposing object in the landscape. In the business parts of the town the streets, though generally rather narrow, are well built, and care has been taken to improve them ... the houses along the principal thoroughfares are generally well built, and have the appearance of respectability and comfort.*

High Street

anticipating his Younger Hall, in St Andrews 12 (see p.130). The TSB, **25-27 East Port**, 1873-5, David MacGibbon, is a scholarly composition in Scots Jacobean. The **Electricity Showroom**, 1938, R H Motion, is 1930s horizontal appliqué. An even greater contrast is the all-metal orieled 13 **Royal Bank of Scotland**, 52 East Port, a design which relates comfortably to the high, glazed, red metal barrel-vault of entrance of 14 **Kingsgate Centre**, 1982-5, Wilson & Womersley. Contrast the rigid oriels of the Dunfermline Building Society, **12 East Port**, 1979-81, James Shearer & Annand.

15 **35-41 East Port**, early 19th century Reminders of a more correct age: rock-faced basements, rusticated ground floors and ashlar 16 upper floors; the **Orient Express** (Colour page C1), 1913, John Fraser, is a well-preserved example of early Art Deco. At the east end of East Port, Rowand Anderson's versatility in church design is demonstrated by the grey, late 17 Gothic **Holy Trinity Episcopal Church**, 1891, with delicate traceried west window and the 18 huge pink neo-Norman **St Margaret's R C Church**, 1889 (being only a fragment of the original design which was to include a circular tower 52m high); chancel, 1936.

19 **Commercial School House**, Commercial School Lane, 1816-17 Expansive five-bay classical block, now flatted, near the more elegant, contemporary three-bay 20 **Viewfield House**, Viewfield Terrace, poised on raised basement and centred on Corinthian doorway and Venetian windows. **Viewfield Terrace**, **Park Avenue** and tree-lined **Comely Park Place** are the addresses of Victorian development which ranged from individual dwellings to semi-detached blockbusters. Although the amenity of this area has been improved by the diversion of traffic on to St Margaret's Drive these large-scale stone houses continue to be taken over as offices.

21 **Erskine Church, Pilmuir Street**, 1798-1800, David Whyte The classical porch, 1897, John Houston, does little to improve the severe ashlar front of this ancient Burgher Chapel. Semicircular gallery on cast-iron columns within.

Above left *Dunfermline Fire Station betrays its Dudok origins.* Above *St Margaret's Church with its unbuilt tower*

22 Dunfermline Fire Station, Carnegie Drive, 1934-6, James Shearer
1930s international style imbued with Scottish quality in a way Sir John Summerson found reminiscent of Mackintosh. The basic composition of horizontal rectangular masses, with the hose-drying tower providing vertical emphasis, is Dutch in influence. Refurbished 1986, Regional Architect.

23 Baths, Pilmuir Street, 1901-5, H J Blanc, and **Clinic**, 1911-12, H & D Barclay, are Carnegie-founded institutions, each reflecting the contemporary belief that public buildings (even industrial buildings such as the nearby **Victoria Works**, 1816) had to be clad in heavy Scots Renaissance garb.

Abbey Parks
A good 18th/19th-century residential area which has resisted redevelopment. The mid 18th-century **2 Abbey Park Place** sports an early 19th-century pilastered doorway; **No 5**, early 19th century, has a slim Doric porch and single-storey wings. Note the square fanlight and panelled quoins; **No 11**, 18th century, mixing crowsteps and quoins features a pilastered pedimented doorway. **Abbey Park House,** *c.*1800, has a north front two storeyed with porch, and south (due to slope of ground) three storeyed with splendid centre bow and balustraded terrace. In **Canmore Street, Nos 27** and **29** have Ionic porticos, **No 4**, 1937, R H Motion ventures into Neo-Symbolist. The office

Abbey Park House

Subtle modelling in brick relieves expansive east elevation of the Alhambra

St Leonard's Parish Church

at **No 2**, *c*.1800, presents the late-Georgian combination of skewputts and columns.

25 **2 Moodie Street**, 18th century
A few steps south of Monastery Street and the Abbey precincts stands the birthplace of Andrew Carnegie, industrialist and benefactor. This restored 18th-century pantiled cottage with swept dormers was once the end of a terrace. Now linked to the **Memorial Building**, 1925, James Shearer, a dramatic contrast with its humble neighbour.

A typical Victorian **Lodge**, 1884, marks the
26 driveway of the **Allan Centre** (former High School), 1883-6, Mercer & Holme. It features a strangely inappropriate four-storey bell tower embedded in a block of Scottish Baronial. At the head of the driveway is the symmetrical **Lauder**
27 **Technical Centre**, 1898-9, H & D Barclay. An elaborate, pedimented entrance bay, flanked by octagonal angle turrets with bellcast roofs has an eastern flavour.

28 **Wilson's Institution**, New Row, 1857, didactic classical, with its pedimented street front, as
29 befitted a school. **Comely Park House**, Head Office of Carnegie UK Trust, dates from 1785 but suffers from 1893 Victorian inflation. Good pyramid sundial, 1785, in the garden. Further up New Row, the brick east elevation of the
30 **Alhambra Cinema**, 1922, reveals a striking vernacular influence.

31 **St Leonard's Parish Church**,
Brucefield Avenue, 1904, P MacGregor Chalmers Plain Romanesque church comprising rubble walls, single side gallery within, and prominent Brechin-style round tower.

St Leonard's Works, Bothwell Street, 1851
Flatted in 1984, this opulent Victorian linen mill was meant to impress. Ionic couple-columned porch, emphasises the entrance on end elevation of three-storey Italianate block eighteen bays long. Recent additions to the harled and crowstepped **The Rhodes**, Bothwell Street, 1695, have failed to hide its good Scottish vernacular origins.

Northern Hospital, Leys Park Road, from 1842
Another classically inspired composition on an institutional scale. It grew out of the austere

Poor House, 1842-3 (now west wing) which in 1905 was extended into a symmetrical façade with baroque centre.

McLean Primary School, Baldbridgeburn, 1895-6, Andrew Scobie
The same Jacobean/Georgian style pioneered 60 years earlier at Madras College, St Andrews (see p.125). Carefully modernised in 1981 by Regional Architect.

Beanstalk Nursery, Blacklaw Road, 1977, Regional Architect
Curved brickwork sliced vertically by window infills; imaginative interior with open playspace.

32**Hill House**, 1623
Excellent three-storey L-plan laird's house with a four-storey bevelled re-entrant tower containing an oval staircase. Interesting details include roll-and-hollow mouldings, typical of late 16th-century Fife, and carved pediments. The entrance at the base of the stair tower has been screened by later additions but the message of pierced letters at the parapet is there for all to see: *Ni Deus Aedificet Domum* (Except the Lord built the house).

Hill House

33**Logie House**, early 19th century; altered 1909, R S Lorimer
An impressive classical spread: the north front offers the extended symmetry of three-storey centre block, two-storey wings, smaller scale two-storey infills, and swagged terminal pavilions. The main feature of the south (garden) front is the three-storey bow flanked by smaller ones.

Pitfirrane

34**Pitfirrane Castle**, 15th century
Dunfermline Golf Club House within oblong tower house, seat of the Halket family, made much more impressive in 1583 when given an additional storey and corbelled turrets, also south wing containing turnpike stair and, as was the custom, a corbelled turret stair serving top storey. Note 16th-century details: a quirked edge roll on jambs and lintels. Extended in 1854 by David Bryce. A vast late 17th-century wing has been demolished and a flat-roofed single-storey extension added.

Hillside House

Wishart

Nether Kinneddar was the home
of William Erskine, Lord Kinneddar
of Session, friend and confidant of
Sir Walter Scott. *'Erskine was the
only name in whose society Scott took
great pleasure.'* (Lockhart's Life).
Scott was a frequent visitor to
Nether Kinneddar and he dedicated
the Third Canto of Marmion to
Erskine.

WEST OF DUNFERMLINE

The hills which lie to the north and west offer
the finest views over the westernmost acres of
the Kingdom. There are the broad plains, the
sheltering belt of the Ochils, the needle-sharp
silhouette of the Wallace Monument in the
middle distance, and, on the horizon, the
mountain ranges by Loch Lomond. The rural
landscape has now repossessed the eruptions of
coalmines, and residential tranquillity has
succeeded the hum of industry. (Colour page C1)
The A823 runs north from Dunfermline, climbs
almost 270m to the gap between Knock and
Wether Hills. At the beginning of the slow
descent it is possible to catch a glimpse of
35 **Hillside House**, a typical 18th-century classical
Scottish mansion later overwhelmed by the
gabled additions reflecting Victorian ambition.
The harled and slated **Hallcroft Farmhouse**,
36 1705, and **Tullohill House**, 1722, preserve
much of their original rugged charm.

SALINE

The character of the buildings and their
attractive gardens lining the steeply sloping
Main Street distinguishes this village. It escaped
the excesses of the industrial developments
which scar neighbouring villages, and although
it supplied some of the labour, it remained rural
in character, cottage-weaving its only industry.

Saline Parish Kirk, 1810, William Stark
An oddity by one of Scotland's finest architects
and master of Playfair (see **Central Glasgow** in
this series). Each of six slim buttressed bays
contains upper and lower windows expressed in
Tudor Gothic. Double corner buttresses at the
west gables, develop into two mini-belfries, one
dummy.

Work of the Mercer family, celebrated local
masons, can be seen in the elaborately capped
gatepiers. Typical of the Main Street are the
Jacobean **Yew** and **Ivy Cottages** (Nos 9 and 11)
whose early 19th-century origins are suggested
by the drip moulds. **Ochil View**, 1851, extended
1901, continues the strong stone tradition with
drip moulds and square-shouldered gables.
Craig House, Oakley Road, a simple
crowstepped block, 1749, commands a
magnificent west view. **Nether Kinneddar**,
37 18th century, is an impressive small mansion
house originally of Georgian design; later
dormers and bay.

Claverley, West Road, 1814-15, situated in pleasant garden, was extended upwards in 1834, and given distinctive carved scroll skewputt.

Left *Saline Parish Church.* Above *Cottage at corner of North Road and Bridge Street.* Centre *Ivy Cottage.* Bottom *Saline Parish Church*

Bridge Street

In addition to crowstepped cottages, c.1800, with large scroll skewputts at **1 & 3 Bridge Street**, there are three contemporary detached two-storey houses of similar symmetrical design: **Smith House** (No 5); **Gateside House** (No 19), with scroll skewputts; and the former manse **Northwood** (No 20), 1795-6, Robert Smith. The former **Free Church**, 1844, Lewis Mercer, is broad-eaved and bargeboarded with arched belfry. In the kirkyard is a quaint, octagonal **Night Watch House**, 1833, with Gothic window. The cottages, **Nos 6,8 & 10**, have been fashioned to their situation, floor levels adjusted to the slope, and a splayed corner, dated 1896. The 18th-century weavers' cottages, originally twelve in all, **20-38 North Road**, provide vivid examples of the right and wrong ways to 38 modernise and preserve.

About 1.5km along the road is **Devonside Farm**, early 19th century, the symmetry of which is emphasised by a central gablet on farmhouse and battlemented wings.

39 **Shieldbank Farm** has an informality about its courtyard buildings one of which is the attractively restored farmhouse **Sandy Dub**, an unusual four bays wide, with a finely moulded doorway dated 1722.

The Minister of Old Parish Church, Carnock, from 1592 to 1646 was **John Row** (1568-1646), the first historian of the Church of Scotland over the period 1558-1637. He is buried in the kirkyard.

CARNOCK and OAKLEY

The village of Gowkhill marks the edge of a rural area which, in the 19th and early 20th centuries, fell prey to the mining industry. Oakley became established with the discovery in 1845 of ironstone. After the demise of iron-working in 1869, the impetus of the succeeding coal rush which sank new mines at Blairhall, 1911, and Comrie, 1936, ensured the continual, mostly unsightly, growth of Oakley and its surrounding villages. Carnock, however, escaped much of the resultant boom.

Carnock

The **Old Inn**, 18th century, is a picturesque whitewashed conglomeration including unobtrusive later additions.

Below Carnock Parish Church. Below right Church of the Most Holy Name – a peaceful rural setting for stained glass jewels. Bottom Carnock Old Parish Church

Carnock Parish Church, 1840, J Henderson Cruciform Romanesque building renovated 1894 by the maverick Stirling architect, J Allan (see **Stirling and the Trossachs** in this series). It lacks the character and historical significance of the **Old Parish Kirk**. Originating from the 13th century, it was rebuilt and repaired in 1602 by Sir George Bruce of Culross, and a study of its windows, aumbry, stoup, even the hooped 17th-century belfry is rewarding. Some fine gravestones and memorials in the kirkyard.

Oakley 'where the people, abandoned by industry, grow old'.

40 **Church of the Most Holy Name**, Oakley, 1956-8, Charles W Gray
Built for (mostly Catholic) miners from Lanarkshire, the interior of this traditional shell of whitewashed harl, crowsteps and stone dressings, sparkles thanks to the magnificent stained glass windows by Gabriel Loire (appropriately from Chartres), who was also responsible for the carved Stations of the Cross, 1967. (Colour page C1)

Inzievar House shows a confident Bryce in full vigour

Arts in Fife

41**Inzievar House**, 1856, David Bryce
Pedimented dormers, finialed bays and
crowstepped gables struggle to maintain balance
in elevations dominated by massive castellated
south-east tower, enlivened by its ogee-roofed
42 angle turret. **West Grange House**, *c*.1760, a
splendid laird's house with two-storey centre
block flanked by single-storey wings. Ground-
floor windows are set within round-headed
arches.

West Grange House

Wishart

43 **Brankstone Grange**, 1864-7, David Bryce;
extended 1896, Rowand Anderson
A home for the elderly, a good site but dreary
architecture: all manner of Baronial features
have been applied to a plain tower core.

McKean

Tulliallan Old Castle (*above*)
The Forth once lapped the walls of 'Tolyalwyns' which Edward I in 1304 ordered to be strengthened. From 15th to 17th centuries it was in the hands of the Blacaders. Sir George Bruce acquired the castle in 1605 and it was inhabited until 1662. By 1820 Admiral George Keith Elphinstone, one of Nelson's officers, had built the new castle.

Tulliallan Old Kirk

Wishart

44 **Tulliallan Old Castle**, from 14th century
A possibly unique survivor in Scotland: an unusually impressive 14th-century hall house protected by moat and portcullis entered through the projecting, semi-octagonal south-west stair tower, in which the chase for the drawbridge chain and portcullis is still quite clear. A similar stair tower projects on the north-west side. The hall, contrary to custom, appears to have been on the ground floor, and the impressive east chamber is comprehensively vaulted with a central pier. It contains elaborate-headed fireplace with carved uprights, flanked by moulded sconces. The vaulting's similarity to that in Glasgow Cathedral may be explained by the castle's occupancy by the Blacader family; Robert Blacader was Archbishop of Glasgow in the late 15th century. Currently under restoration by John Reid for the Mitchell Trust.

KINCARDINE on FORTH
The extreme west tip of the Kingdom offers a bridge across the Forth, two enormous electric generating stations and an army of giant pylons bestriding the countryside. Founded as a Burgh of Barony on reclaimed marshland in 1663, Kincardine became a major port and centre of ship-building and servicing, salt and papermaking and quarrying.

Tulliallan Parish Church,
Kirk Street, 1832-3, George Angus
Gothic with double-gabled east front, and five-

stage clocktower – a close copy of his Kettle
Parish Church (see p.90). The west tower of the
Old Parish Kirk, 1675, deroofed after the
present church was built, has distinctive flared
pyramidal roof and contains some excellent
classical detailing. Note particularly the
pilastered doorway and pedimented armorial
panel (*right*).

Tulliallan Castle, 1817-20, William Atkinson
A large symmetrical castellated mansion in 'toy
town' style – lightly buttressed entrance tower
with Gothic traceried windows, ponderous
battlements and slender corner turrets with
loopholes. Scottish Police College since 1954
with vast extensions.

Kincardine Bridge, 1932-6,
Alexander Gibb & Partners
Unexciting lattice steel structure spanning
concrete piers, whose approach roads carved up
and almost mortally wounded Kincardine.
Patches survive. The plain, regular fenestration
with margins of **Kirk Street** bear all the
characteristics of the 18th century: **No 52** is
dated 1778, and **No 24**, 1722. There are classical
doorways at **Nos 18** and **20**, and the scroll
skewputt detail is much repeated.

High Street
On the east side sober 19th-century fronts face
the 17th-century **Mercat Cross**, with its
octagonal shaft and moulded capital.
No 26 Keith Street, late 18th century, stylish
wallhead gablet with key-blocked window and
scroll skewputts; **Nos 32-34 & 54** are similar.
Ye Old House, Forth Street, 1734, is homely in
its black and white inn finish.

Excise Street and **Cooper's Lane** have the
makings of an attractive precinct. **Nos 3 & 5
Excise Street**, 1745, were rebuilt in the 19th
century with pedimented and curved dormer
windows. **Nos 10-24**, 18th century, form an
excellent group combining traditional features
and finishes. Opposite, the more recent **Nos 7-13**
make a pleasing contrast and the **Unicorn
Hotel**, a considerably altered 18th-century
coaching inn, is not out of keeping.

Top *Pilastered doorway displays
classical detail.* Centre and bottom
Typical datestones in Kincardine

The crowstepped **6 Cooper's Lane**, 1750, was
once a Roman Catholic Chapel.

The Orchard, 24 Kilbagie Street, probably

The **Unicorn Hotel**, Kincardine,
was the birthplace of Sir James
Dewar, 1842-1923, physicist and
inventor of the vacuum flask.

18th century, has a skewputt dated 1629, and an inscribed stone on gable. **Nos 36-44** and **60 Primrose Villas**, also dating from the 18th century, similarly feature scroll skewputts. Kincardine now treasures its date stones, which sometimes appear incongruously on 20th-century housing, e.g. Station Road. They can also add confusion: as at **Kincardine House**, 10 Walker Street (now flatted) where the backdoor lintel is dated 1720 and the first-floor lintels 1700 and 1664. Of less historic pretension, but significantly greater style, is the striking mansion **Burnbrae**, *c.*1800, of classical symmetry and detail.

West and east of the town stand the industrial [45]structures of **Kincardine Power Station**, [46]opened 1960, and **Longannet Power Station**,

Top *Scroll skewputt with sundial.* Centre *Kincardine Power Station viewed from the south bank of the Forth.* Below *Blair Castle*

opened 1966. Both designed by Robert Matthew, Johnson-Marshall & Partners, the latter station, with its gigantic four-bayed generating hall, flat and serrated roofed ancillary blocks and, above all, 180m four-flued stack, is similar to the Cockenzie design by the same firm.

[47]**Blair Castle**, early 19th century
Now Carlaw Convalescent Home for Miners, it was built on a heroic classical scale, with giant coupled Ionic pilasters.

[48]**Dunimarle Castle**, *c.*1840, R & R Dickson
The Dicksons subordinated an 18th-century two-storey house on an ancient castle site to a three-storey new block at right angles, with an overbearing, four-storey circular tower and stair round complete with corbelled balconies and crenellated parapets. This strangely disparate

composition was once the focal point of dramatic landscaping.

CULROSS

The captivating irregularity of the wynds and the informality of its buildings, the brightness of the whitewashed harl and the warmth of the pantiles, the pleasing texture of the high dykes and cobbled wynds – all (as many film directors have discovered) make Culross a photogenic environment for the 17th and 18th centuries.

Some historians lament the loss of the original wide medieval streets and stress that few houses are older than the 17th century when, during the golden age of the Royal Burgh (Charter 1588) much rebuilding took place and 'inferior' pantile roofing was used. Until the National Trust for Scotland instituted its programme of restoration in 1932, time in Culross had stood still for almost 150 years and thereby ensured its future.

Arts in Fife

Dunimarle Castle

At the **Old Parish Church** the lintels above the north and south doors (formed in the 17th century) were made out of gravestones – hence the carved crosses and swords lying horizontally.

The Study – the essence of Culross

Wishart

Culross Abbey, from 13th century (*above*)
This Cistercian abbey founded by Malcolm, Earl of Fife, in 1217 contained choirs east and west of the rood screen. After the screen, the pulpitum and side walls were strengthened by Abbot Andrew Masoun (1498-1513), the sturdy tower complete with newelstair at north-west angle was built on top and a new entrance was made from the west side (the crenellated parapet replaced original saddle-back roof in 1823). Of the west choir for the lay-brothers (abandoned *c*.1500) only the south wall remains. The east (monastic) choir and transepts became part of the **Parish Church**, in 1633, modified by William Stirling in 1824 and comprehensively restored in 1905 by Rowand Anderson. The **Bruce Vault**, 1642, contains a fine Renaissance

Wishart

Bottom Culross c.1680 by Capt. John Slezer. Palace and Abbey on the right horizon

The 17th-century, two-storey block of **Culross Abbey House** (*below*) built by Edward, first Lord Bruce of Kinloss (forebears of Earls of Elgin) was the first Scottish house of any size to show Renaissance influence; c.1670 an additional storey was provided and the wings raised to four-storey corner towers.

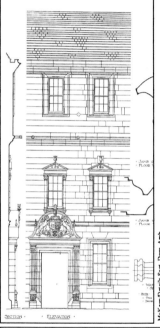

McKean/Details Scot. Dom. Arch.

mural monument to Sir George Bruce by John Mercer of Carnock, including effigies of Sir George and his wife and the delightful kneeling figures of their eight children.

The steeply sloping site necessitated (as at Dunfermline Abbey see p.9) substantial undercrofts in order to provide a level cloister. Only traces survive of the undercrofts of the east and west ranges (monks' quarters). At the south end of the west range (occupied by the lay brothers) vaulted sections are exposed. The lower, a kitchen at undercroft level, is plain, but the lay-brothers' frater above comprises three vaulted bays, and there are indications of the dorter above. A stone sewer can still be seen in the kitchen. Adjacent to the frater is a vaulted transe (linking cloister to outer court) where monks could meet 'outsiders'.

The **Manse**, 1637, was built when the north part of the west range was removed. A west wing, 1824, William Stirling, made it an L-plan although the circular tower at re-entrant angle is 17th century.

Culross Abbey House, 1608, enlarged 1670 Its original magnificence is best appreciated from John Slezer's engraving of 1693 which also illustrates its extensive formal gardens. By c.1800 it was in ruins; reconstruction by Sir Robert Preston followed in 1830, and in 1954-6 Robert Hurd & Partners redesigned it to a smaller scale. The classical aedicular first-floor windows on the north front were carefully preserved and the ogee-roofed pavilions were retained albeit single-storeyed.

McKean/Slezer

Parley Hill House, early 18th century
A glance at its curvilinear west gable with scroll
skewputts and two oval windows explains its
nickname 'House of the Evil Eyes'.

Along a grassy track, about 0.5km north-west is
49 **Old Parish Church**, abandoned 16th century.
Of the original pre-Reformation building only
the lower part of a lancet window on the south
side remains.

Town House, 1626
In the 17th century, the Forth came up to the
edge of the road. Today the Sandhaven has been
reclaimed and grassed and makes a good setting
for the Town House. In 1783, its elevation
assumed its present (almost) symmetrical form:
a two-way forestair was provided and its
powerful clocktower made to rise abruptly, all
quoined and ogival-roofed, from a wallhead
shorn of dormers.

Wishart

Abutting its west gable is the **Tron House**, 18th
century, with corniced doorway on the west
front. The **House** attached to the rear, **Myrtle
Bank** (rubble stone and scroll skewputt) and
Mintlea (harled with exposed margins) form an
attractively restored group of buildings. Note
most houses in Culross are simply named or are
identified by their owner's name; e.g. the 17th-
century harled and pantiled **R Milne House**
with stair tower at rear and **J Robertson
House** which presents a magnificent eight-
window and door gable end complete with wall-
mounted sundial. **Tron Shop**, 18th century, has
window, door and forestair redesigned to suit
the traditional pattern.

The **Tolbooth** (*above*) is a regular
feature of old Fife towns. In this
medieval building the Town Council
and Burgh Court met. Here taxes were
paid, weights, measures and Royal
Records were kept and prisoners
held (cells were generally on the
ground floor). The stone platform
opposite Culross Town House marks
the **Tron** – the public weighbeam.

The Palace

The Palace, from 16th century (Colour page C1)
The development of The Palace, a unique
example of merchant's house of the period,
appropriately marks the increasing prosperity of
Sir George Bruce, its owner. Wedged in the
middle of the west range, facing the street is the
16th-century unpretentious three-storey original
dwelling. Its richly carved wallhead dormers
(with rounded margins) still exist – the centre
one is initialled GB and dated 1597. Later 17th-
century accommodation, north and south, is
reached by turnpike and forestair respectively.
A later north block with stable buildings to the
east (including dormered hayloft) completes the
characteristic view of The Palace. This range
provides only accommodation and its wallhead

Wishart

Wishart

'Croon o' the Cassie'. 'Croon for the Quality'; the lower sides for the 'less exalted'

17th century Culross industries included coalmining (Sir George Bruce succeeded the monk owners), saltmaking, quarrying, hand-loom weaving. James IV had also granted the monopoly of girdle making – round iron baking plates of which it was said *'I'll gar yer lugs ring like a Culross girdle'*. All were doomed. The mines flooded in 1625, the Carron ironworks (opened in 1760) captured the girdle trade and in the 19th century the power-looms of Dunfermline made the hand-loom redundant.

Sir George Bruce, d.1625, was foremost salt manufacturer and colliery owner of the 17th century. It is claimed that he introduced the endless chain and bucket system (horse-drawn) to drain the mines and he is credited with being the first to sink a pit under the sea. A Royal inspection of the Culross mine ended with a shout of *'Treason!'* when James VI found himself surfacing on an island. Bruce hastily assured him that a boat awaited his return journey to the mainland but the King returned via the mine. One of the features of his 'Palace' at Culross was the first-floor strongroom of fireproof construction – vaulted ceiling, tiled floor over vaulted ground floor, extra thick walls and double door. In 1600 he bought Gedeleth and renamed it Broomhall, the Earl of Elgin's ancestral home.

dormers are pedimented, initialled SGB (now knighted!) and dated 1611. The group is a picturesque texture of whitewash, stone, pantile and steep pitched crowstepped gables. Internally, the prime features are contemporary tempera-painted walls and ceilings.

Nearby, **Bessie Bar's Hall** (it was her malthouse), 1776, has a broad forestair on its street gable, while, across the road, is the contemporary, restored **Bessie Bar House** with sympathetic modern pend.

At West Green the rubble **Marshall House**, 18th century, has interesting lugged architraved doorway dated 1636. The harled **I Muir House**, 17th century, looks across the Green to **Balgownie House** (Inchkeith Private School), *c*.1840, a plain classic mansion in six bays. On the shore, is its unusual barrel-vaulted **boathouse**, 19th century.

East and north of Tron House on **Back Causeway, Ferguson's House** (with forestair), **Ingleneuk** and **Rowan Bank** (although altered) are said to date from the late 17th century. All the old roads lead to **The Cross**, an open space irregular in shape, uneven of surface. The shaft and head capped with a unicorn of the **Mercat Cross** are by J W Small, 1902. The octagonal base set in cobbles dates from *c*.1600. Forming the south-west border of The Cross is the piended pantiled gable of **House** on the corner of Mid Causeway, the plain screenwall with opening, and the attractive crowstepped gable (with assorted windows) of **House** on the corner of Back Causeway, dated 1577, and alleged to be the oldest house in the Burgh.

The Study, 1633 (Colour page C1)
Outstanding three-storey house with swept wallhead dormers and a dramatic four-storey jamb containing in its corbelled top storey the study itself with its own swept dormers and corbelled angle round. Note the original style of the windows, here and at The Palace: fixed leaded glass upper sash with wood shuttered opening below.

Next door at **No 2 Tanhouse Brae**, 17th century, the projecting bay has deeply moulded jambs and lintels and a Greek inscription. The 17th-century **Nos 3,4** and **5** form another picturesque group, here built to suit the brae.

Note the panel on the Butcher's House, 1664, containing cleaver and sharpener.

On the other side the **Coachman's Cottage**, Kirk Street, 1670, restored 1950s, has an early 19th-century pilastered doorway while **Snuff Cottage**, 1763, and inscribed *wha wad ha' thocht it* in round-headed window, has key-blocked doorway. Taking advantage of slope **Shoemaker's Cottage** has a laigh floor; the lintel of the access door is dated 1669.

At The Cross, on the corner of Little and Mid Causeway, is **The Ark**, a 17th-century sturdy building believed, at one time, to be a sailors' hostel. On **Little Causeway** is **House**, 1609, with unusual ledged street gable. Next door the **Nunnery**, *c.*17th century, which takes its name from veiled head carved on skewputt, has irregular plan and typical improvised roof with leanto over forestair. Another attractive group is at **Mid Causeway** where **Nos 5** and **7** (Bishop Leighton's House), early 17th century, have been reconstructed out of three houses, and linked with the more modest 18th-century dwellings at **Nos 9** and **11**.

The character of **Low Causeway** has been diluted by insensitive alterations and modern intrusions but **The Haven**, 1623, retains much of its original appearance and care has been taken with the recent restoration of **R W Alexander House**, 18th century. **St Kentigern's**, an early 19th-century villa, sits immaculately detached with classical front complete with full-height pilastered ends.

50To the east, the single-storey **Valleyfield Endowment**, 1830 and recently restored, remains impressive with dominating central pediment and armorial panel.

TORRYBURN
On the west approach to High Valleyfield is the 51bizarre **Woodhead** Farmhouse, early 19th century, with Georgian symmetry, classical doorway and Gothic windows. Later flintstone embellishment.

Landed properties, such as Valleyfield and Torrie, were sacrificed for the exploitation of coal. Mining communities, Low and High Valleyfield, Newmills, and Low Torry, began to cluster along the coastline. Torryburn itself, like Saline, managed to keep much of its original rural

'God provides and will provide'

The Study at Culross
The lower room is full of objects history's ordered bric-à-brac in which visitors inherently bored show intelligent interest

The upper room is still empty there (in that small cartesian cell) remains the merest chance for the essential to happen

Kenneth White from 'Handbook for the Diamond Country'

The encrusted entrance to Woodhead Farmhouse

In 1822, Alison Cunningham, the nurse of Robert Louis Stevenson was born at **Torryburn.** Of her he wrote, when he dedicated to her his children's Garden of Verses: *'My second mother, my first wife The angel of my infant life'.* From her he imbibed his interest in Scots history possibly including the **witch-mania,** resulting in the burning or drowning of the victim, which was prevalent in the Torryburn area. Unusually, the last victim, Lilias Adie, died in prison in 1704.

charm but the rest suffered the ravages of rapid development, particularly during the late 19th-century influx of miners, and the subsequent desolation when the pits finally closed.

Blairhall – birthplace of Sir William Bruce of Kinross

52 **Blairhall,** off A985, is a late 17th century laird's house – plain five bay front symmetrical about moulded doorway; 20th-century pinnacled gateway in keeping; all beautifully rescued by Marcus Dean.

Torryburn Parish Church, dated 1800; reconditioned 1928. The corbelled belfry and external stair make a plain Gothic block more interesting.

On shoreside stands **Craigflower,** a radical remodelling of an earlier house by David Bryce, 1862, converted to flats in 1985. It contains all the elements of his Scottish Baronial: asymmetry, crowstepped gables punctuated by angle turrets, finials and pedimented dormers, corbelled transformation from angle to round and from bay to square.

Ship Cottage doorway

On **Low Causeway,** 18th century harled, pantiled, crowstepped **Lilac Cottages** and **Nos 4** and **4a** retain much of their original character while **3 Ship Cottage,** 1745, restored 1887, is more formal with moulded eaves course, classical doorway (keystone, 1745) and, above, ship carved on panel, 1747. In **Main Street, Low Torry,** both **81** (Rockvale) and **91** (Ellenbank) are 18th-century two-storey buildings of symmetrical design but differing detail.

On **Main Street, Newmills,** the 19th-century castellated gateway, and flanking arches and attached Gothic **Lodge** are reminders of Torrie 53 Estate. Also, off A985, its **stables,** *c.*1785 – castellated with substantial corner towers.

54 **Pitliver,** a large mansion dating from *c.*1625, features a central four-storey stair tower. In the 18th century, the house was extended west and north. The cryptic inscription on the gable referring to Wellwood (owners 1733-1920) was added in the 19th century when a Victorian flourish took the form of a large square tower (corbelled, castellated and ornate entrance) built against original tower.

The village of **Charlestown** arose from a commercial decision by Charles, the 5th Earl of Elgin. Coal and limestone were on his estate and the harbour gave ready access to the sea routes. What was needed was accommodation for the workers, a processing plant and overland transport – hence the creation of the village, the limekilns and the railway, first powered by horses then steam. The complex became the most extensive limeworks in the country but after a life of almost two centuries economics dictated its closure in 1937.

CHARLESTOWN

Charlestown was a model village created *c.*1770 by Charles, 5th Earl of Elgin (1732-71), and the monogram of his initials can still be traced in its layout. Of the terraces of harled houses, slated and pantiled, the simplest designs were built first, e.g. in **Double Row.** Later designs, e.g. **North Row,** *c.*1820, were more pretentious. Today, despite numerous alterations, the original concept can still be appreciated. The focal point is the Baronial **Queen's Hall,** 1887, by Rowand Anderson.

The Old Granary, Rock Road, *c.*1800, was once a handsome block containing stables on the ground floor, railway manager's flat on the first and granary on the second. Now the ground floor accommodates a shop. Opposite one of the old saltpans on Harbour Road is the delightful **Easter Cottage,** *c.*1760. At the recessed centre bay the roof is swept up in segmental form and supported on two slim 'sprouting' columns to form a portico. Further west are the remains of the *dark, grey, dirty* range of **limekilns,** *c.*1780, cut into the cliff face. The simple arched rubble openings lead to the grimly impressive vaulted interior.

Centre *The Rows, Charlestown.*
Above *Easter Cottage*

Above *Hope Cottage and detail of sundial.* Right *King's Cellar*

LIMEKILNS

About 1km east of Charlestown is Limekilns, once another centre of a variety of industries. In addition to limeworks there were brewing, fishing and fish curing, salt, soap and ropemaking – even shipbuilding. Its **Harbour** (originally the port for medieval Dunfermline) was its main asset. In the 16th century stone pier replaced the timber one. (**Brucehaven Harbour**, *c*.1750, was built specially for the coal trade.) Today, as in Charlestown with which it is increasingly linked, it has become an attractive place for retirement and a dormitory for commuters.

For a village church the severe classical style of **Limekilns Parish Church**, Church Street, 1825, comes as a surprise, especially the scale of the detail: two-storey pilasters supporting full-width pediment.

The King's Cellar may be dated from the 1362 Charter and certainly in the 14th century the monks of Dunfermline stored wines and other imports at Limekilns. After being a store the Cellar became a School (Academy), a library, an Episcopal Chapel and now a Masonic Lodge. The discovery of a kiln at the west end of the building suggested bottle manufacture for wines.

King's Cellar, early 16th century

The earliest relic of Limekilns' trading history is this splendid historic storehouse dominating **Academy Square**. The pediment, 1581, is thought to have been brought from Abbot's House, Dunfermline, by its owner Robert Pitcairn, influential Commendator of Dunfermline. It is of barrel-vaulted construction, half-round on lower floor, pointed in upper floor where it 'springs' almost from floor level. Remnants of turnpike at the north-east angle suggest at one time a higher floor or tower. In 1911 it was restored and forestair added by F W Deas. The adjacent **Oriel House**, 18th century, suffers from poor later additions.

Nos 4,5, 6 and **7 Academy Square**, 18th century, are more modest but remain more attractive – likewise the 18th-century **11 Hope**

Cottage and **26 Main Street** both carefully renovated, the former having sundial dated 1689. At **Halket's Hall** some 18th-century houses have retained attractive features: the swept wallhead dormers at **No 5**, the margined windows at **No 11**, the moulded eaves at **No 13** dated 1774.

Along the shore only the east gable with two lancet windows and part of the north wall 55 remain of **Old Rosyth Church**, late 16th century, but originally dating from the 13th century.

Broomhall

56 **Broomhall**, 1796-7, Thomas Harrison Residence of the Earl of Elgin, presiding over Limekilns and Charlestown and enjoying extensive views over the Forth. Despite a mountain of drawings of proposed modifications prepared at various times by over a dozen distinguished architects, Harrison's calm neoclassical mansion – a recasting of a 1702 house – has survived relatively unscathed. The south front of the two-storey centre block consists of eleven bays, the centre three being in the form of a bow; note coupled Ionic pilasters on lower storey. Both this centre block and single-storey flanking wings with unusual re-entrant quadrants are on a raised basement. The classical portico on the north front is by Thomson & Wilson in 1865-6.

ROSYTH
When, in 1903, the Admiralty began the construction of the Dockyard, Rosyth was planned as a 'garden city' to house the workers.

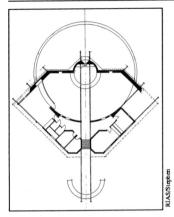

The informal layout proceeded on Ebenezer Howard rules – central park, encircling housing, peripheral industry – but now only the housing in tree-lined avenues is significant, e.g. the pleasant designs in **Queensferry Road**, 1919, A H Mottram and Grey & Fairbairn – harled, slated with gablets and swept dormers. On Hilton Road the **Anglican Church of St Margaret**, 1968-9, MOW Architects, features a dramatic keel-shaped roof. **St John's Primary School**, Heath Road, 1989, by the Regional Architect is fashionable with low-pitched roofs and meticulous details.

INVERKEITHING

Old Inverkeithing (its walls and four ports were removed in the 16th century) stands on a small plateau on a hillside where the distinctive squat busy tower of St Peter's Kirk can be seen from all approach roads. It achieved Royal Burgh status in 1165. Paper-making remains the major local source of employment, the once thriving shipbreaking industry is now little more than an ugly blot on the quayside.

Top James F Stephen's RIAS competition-winning plan for S.S Peter & Paul R.C. church at HMRNB Rosyth, with its dramatic entrance. Top right Anglican Church of St Margaret. Lower right and above Garden City Housing, Rosyth

Inverkeithing Parish Church, St Peter's,
1826, J Gillespie Graham
Plain Gothic revival nave and aisles, pruned in 1900 by MacGregor Chalmers. The main feature is the 14th-century short, angle-buttressed

square tower through which passes the entrance. Its corbelled parapet is 16th century, its spire 1835 and the very Victorian clock gables 1883.

Fordell's Lodging, 16-18 Church Street, c.1670 Copybook example for 19th-century Scottish Baronialists: steep-pitched, crowstepped gables, wallhead dormers, and corbelled turret with conical roof.

Tolbooth, Townhall Street, 1754-70 The pepperpot belfry seems at odds with the quoins and pedimented tower 1754-5; the three-storey block complete with classical detail followed in 1770.

Rosebery House, 9 King Street (nicknamed 'Toofal' as roof is lean-to), has window details and vaulted basements which suggest 16th-century origin but alterations and additions in the 17th and 18th centuries have given it a Georgian appearance. **No 2-4 Bank Street**, the impressive **Thomsoun's House**, 1617, restored 1965, complete with caphoused stair tower. The splendid moulded doorway has carved inscribed pediment with thistle finial and scrolls. The elaborate **Mercat Cross** stands at the junction of **Bank Street** and **High Street** – a reputedly 16th-century octagonal shaft with four-shielded capital. In 1688 a sundial and unicorn were added (Colour page C2).

Top *Inverkeithing Tolbooth.* Centre and above *Thomsoun's House with inscribed pediment.* Left *Town House of the Hendersons of Fordell drawn by McGibbon & Ross*

35

Top *Inverkeithing Tolbooth with Mercat Cross in original location c.1910.* Above *Inverkeithing Friary.* Below *Mercat Cross in present location with Thomsoun's House behind*

The narrow north end of **High Street** contains two early 19th-century painted façades. At **No 8** the shop has Edwardian stained-glass upper lights and curved window at south-west; **No 10**, *c.*1800, is more classical with rusticated quoins, dentilled cornice and scroll skewputts. One of the houses rebuilt after the ravages of Cromwell's army was **14-18 High Street, Providence House**, which contains excellent classical doorway on the street gable, dated 1688.

Friary, Queen Street, from 14th century
Now an architectural confusion, around a core formed from the north-west wing of a Franciscan convent; remodelled as a tenement in the 17th century. The lower apartments are barrel vaulted while the upper floor, converted to a museum in 1974, is reached by a forestair introduced in a reconstruction by J Wilson Paterson, 1932-4. The forbidding rubble walls and small windows are offset by the pleasant Friary Garden in which cellars and other traces of the original convent can be seen.

The street front of **2 Hope Street** (former Corn Exchange, later Drill Hall) is almost Palladian in its simplicity.

Inverkeithing Railway Station is one of the few late 20th-century replacements in Fife – its simple relaxed design and landscaping merits attention and commendation.

Inverkeithing High School,
1982, Regional Architect
Occupying a sloping site to the north of town, it wears the inevitable busy appearance of a functional complex – the most striking feature being a massive stilted circular unit with tentacle links to the main block.

57**Fordell Castle**, 16th century
Simple and logical from a planning point of view – a fortified block, four storeys high, stairways at north-west and south-east angles and conical-roofed turrets at north-east and south-west angles. Each main stair has small turret stair extension on top chamber. The ground floor is vaulted; the upper floors generally divided into two ensuite apartments. Externally, this simple arrangement has been transformed into an exciting archetypal castle. The south-east stair wing, with a slight corbel, rises to a caphouse.

Fordell Castle

The north-west wing is corbelled out, taken in, and then a ponderous three-stage corbel supports a crenellated parapet which encloses the lookout and embraces the turret stair (with conical roof), c.1855. The south elevation has three neat wallhead dormers.

Fordell Chapel, 1650, is Renaissance in symmetry, Gothic in detail – the exception being the corniced doorway with rusticated surround. The later belfry has crenellated spired appearance of a scaled-down church tower.

St Bridget's Church – history unfolding in a linear pattern

58 **St Bridget's Church**, Dalgety Bay
Consecrated 1244
At the east end of the shore, the most unusual feature of this church is the large addition – almost a tower house – of 1610 at the west

gable, which contained burial vaults on the ground floor and commodious laird's loft and retiring room on the upper floor. When at the end of the 17th century, galleries were inserted at the ends of the nave, access to the west gallery was from the laird's loft and the fore stair on the east gable was built to serve the east gallery. The two-stone arched head to doorway on the south front suggests 16th-century work.

DALGETY BAY

The fortunes of the old parish of Dalgety were bound up with coal from the Fordell Pit and its export from St David's Harbour. Its steep decline ended in 1962 when construction of Scotland's first privately built new town began. Today although largely a dormitory for Edinburgh it supports a lively industrial estate.

Dalgety Kirk, 1830, J Gillespie Graham
A small oblong in Gothic mullion-and-transom style. Between the two churches, on the crest of the hill, stands the former manse. **Ardhmor**, *c.*1830, J Gillespie Graham. Originally a Georgian design on raised basement. In 1897-8 it acquired dormers and bays.

No longer is there a **Donibristle House** but at the west end of the shore remain, in poor condition, the two plain but substantial (three storeys by seven bays) **service wings**, *c.*1720, Alexander McGill, flanking stately stairway which climbed to the grand forecourt. Even today the scale is impressive. Related buildings include the once elegant **chapel**, 1729-32, Alexander McGill, with Gibbs' surrounds to openings and commanding belfry. The **stables**, 18th century, have been transformed, 1988, Muir Group, into private dwellings. The mansarded ranges form an attractive courtyard with pend entry marked by stylish octagonal drum complete with dome and lantern.

Top *Upmarket refurbishment of Donibristle Stables.* Above *William Adam's design for Donibristle from* Vitruvius Scoticus. Right *Fortronic*

The shore of Donibristle Castle, in 1592, witnessed the murder of the Protestant Earl of Moray by the Catholic Earl of Huntly. Some say he was prompted by James VI who, in addition to his political ploys, had his suspicions which had been bruited in the ballad:

*'He was a braw gallant
Ane he played at the gluve
And the bonny Earl of Moray
Oh, he was the Queen's luve'.*

The castle was burnt down, then rebuilt *c.*1700, visited by Defoe in 1724 and burned down again in 1858.

Modern materials and manufacturing processes in the industrial estate are reflected in its architecture, e.g. **Fortronic**, 1983-4, Wylie

Shanks – an eye-catching, all-embracing
aluminium structure covered with vivid orange
sheet-steel panels separated by brown gaskets.
    North of the railway and the busy coast road
is a quiet rural paradise around Otterston Loch.

Cockairnie House

59 **Cockcairnie House**, from 16th century
    Tall and broad (three storeys plus attics by six
    bays), whitewashed with stone margins. The
    60 small pedimented porch is *c*.1835. **Couston
    Castle**, originally built in the 14th century, was
    vandalised by 1985, then rescued in award-
    winning style by Ian Begg, 1986-8. Its 16th-
    century form has been carefully recreated,
    including stair turret at re-entrant of L-plan.

ABERDOUR
Aberdour, 'at the mouth of the Dour', was once,
like Anstruther, in two parts – Wester, a Burgh
of Barony, 1501, and Easter, a Burgh of
Regality, 1638. The late 16th-century **gateway**
to Aberdour Castle, classically corniced with
gunloops, was relocated post-railway in 1890.

Aberdour Castle evolves palatially

Aberdour Castle, from 14th century
Seat of the Douglas Earls of Morton, on a strong

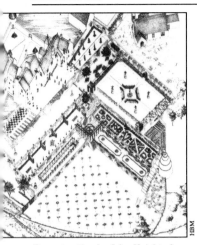

Reconstruction by John Knight of Aberdour Castle and formal gardens as they might have been c.1575

defensive position on east bank of the Dour Burn, offers gracious relics of a magnificent aristocratic pile. Of the 14th-century massive tower house at the north-west corner (reconstructed with vaulted ground floor in the 15th century) only the south gable survives above first-floor level. The 16th-century Renaissance extension, with turnpike link at the north-west angle and stair tower at south-west, is still identifiable. Note vaulted kitchen with cavernous flue. In the 17th century, another range, added to the east of the 16th-century block, includes two towers in the north and, at re-entrant angle formed by square, gabled south wing, a turnpike stair within a squat square tower. Now restored, it has stables on the ground floor, a long gallery on the upper floor and custodian's house in the south wing. The **walled garden** contains a pedimented gateway, 1632. South of the castle, four impressive terraces, said to date from 1570, are being restored. The large beehive-shaped **doocot**, 16th century, is one of only five left in Fife.

Right *St Fillan's Kirk.* Below *Interior*

St Fillan's Kirk, Kirk Wynd, from 1140
'Just to enter St Fillan's is to worship'. Small, rectangular church whose Romanesque nave and chancel were built c.1140. The simple chancel survives, a joy to behold. The aisle, necessitating the formation of the fine arcade, and the porch were added c.1500. Later additions included the 16th-century Gothic window in the west gable, the sturdy belfry with pyramid roof, 1588, and the north aisle (now used by choir) in 1608. Neglected, it was deroofed c.1790, and derelict until restored with care in 1926 by W Williamson (Colour page C2).

Wishart

Aberdour House, from 17th century
18th-century gateway piers, with fluted
alternate courses and ball finials, lead to the
architecturally schizophrenic house on the west
bank of Dour Burn, opposite the Castle. Early
17th-century handsome, crowstepped, U-plan
block where end bays project with piended roofs;
the swept dormers of the gabled main roof are
unusually splayed. The unrelated classical
north-west block was applied c.1731.

*Original 17th-century aspect of
Aberdour House*

High Street
The palatial **East Entrance Gateway**, 1870,
Brown & Wardrop, used to lead to St Colme
House; now serves only a private housing estate.
Opposite, **Woodside Hotel,** 1879, W L Moffat,
has a tall château-type faceted roof of fish-scale
slating. **Nos 1,2,3,4 West High Street,** late
18th century, are a pleasant group of traditional
houses with neat timber porches. **No 6 Sands
Place,** 1713, features a forestair. Nearer the
burgh boundary, is a 17th/18th-century circular
doocot with lean-to roof.

Seabank House, Shore Road,
c.1835, possibly by Thomas Hamilton
Massive villa distinguished by the central
cluster of octagonal flues which rises from the
low-pitched, wide-eaved roof.

61Off the A987 **The Murrel,** 1908, Frank Deas, an
exceptionally picturesque Arts & Crafts house
for the architect himself; imaginatively
landscaped.

Frank Deas, architect and close
friend and confidant of Sir Robert
Lorimer, who regularly spent
weekends at his house, The Murrel,
near Aberdour. Deas helped
Christopher Hussey in the
preparation of *The Work of Sir
Robert Lorimer,* 1931.

Wishart

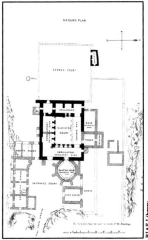

GROUND PLAN

RIAS Library

18th-century view by Clerk of Eldin

INCHCOLM

If the tide is suitable, it is possible to sail from 18th-century Aberdour Harbour to Inchcolm, sometimes described as the 'Iona of the East'. A primitive pointed barrel-vaulted **Hermit's Cell** – slabbed roof restored 14th/15th century – is a relic of the early inhabitants.

The **Church**, early 12th century, comprised a plain nave and chancel. A new choir was built at the end of the 12th century, and further extended in the 13th. At the same time, with the establishment of the Abbey, status granted 1223, the Chapter House was built and cloister set out. (Unusually perhaps, because level space on island was limited, its open courtyard is small and eventually the monks walked, sheltered from the wind and waves, in the barrel-vaulted ground-floor galleries of the east,

RCAHMS

south and west ranges.) As was later to happen at Culross Abbey, a 13th-century square tower (here slightly crenellated on moulded corbels) was built on suitably strengthened rood screen and pulpitum. In the 14th century the introduction of barrel vault within nave and chancel facilitated a horizontal division into north cloister walk with Abbot's lodging above. Exploration of the relics of the conventual buildings reveals alterations and additions which began almost 800 years ago and continued for over four centuries. The most complete, and best designed, is the 13th-century **Chapter House** – octagonal in plan with buttresses on exposed angles. It is rib-vaulted and entrance from cloister is finely moulded. Directly above is the 14th-century **Warming House** with pointed barrel-vault. The steep pyramid roof forms a pleasing counterpoint with the tower. All the upper floors of the cloister ranges are pointed barrel vaults – the dorter in the east range is linked to reredorter at the south end, the frater in west range has dais and pulpitum bay (as at Dunfermline) and kitchen at the west end.

62 **Easterheughs**, from 1946, William Thomas Amazing tower house in 16th-century form, built gradually, over 20 years, by occupant using material salvaged from other buildings including Otterstone House; engagingly underscaled although perfectly proportioned.

63 **Newbigging**, 1825, is an unpretentious laird's house, with pilastered door and single-storey wings; 17th-century lectern doocot nearby.

For three days the hermit who lived on **Inchcolm** gave succour to Alexander I when he was stormbound in 1123. On his deliverance the King vowed he would found an Augustinian Priory in honour of St Columba. After his death, c.1124, his brother, David I, generously endowed the new monastery. Although much of the first foundation is in ruins subsequent work including the magnificent Chapter House and, above, the Warming House or Scriptorium (where Abbot Bower is said to have written his sequel to Fordun's *Scotichronicon*) still remain. For this remarkable preservation the island's relative isolation offers an explanation although in 1581 Edinburgh Town Council gave permission to remove *'thackstane and ashlar for the Tolbooth'*.

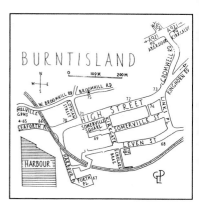

BURNTISLAND
Its *raison d'être* was a good natural harbour,

Late 17th-century maritime view of Burntisland by Captain John Slezer

which, through the centuries, was used for fishing, trade (particularly the export of coal in the last quarter of the 19th century), ferry terminal (until the opening of the Forth Bridge in 1890) and shipbuilding (during the Second World War 69 ships were built). The British Aluminium Company now provides the main industry

Wishart

St Columba's (*above*) – '*built four-square to demonstrate equality of all believers*' – was the first church built in Scotland after the Reformation. Archbishop Laud noted that there was '*no place for altar*'. Here, in 1601, in the presence of James VI, the new translation of the Bible was proposed.

Right *Interior view*

RCAHMS

As early as AD 83 Agricola is said to have chosen Burntisland as a naval base. James V made it a Royal Burgh in 1541 – '*We have built and repaired the harbour formerly called Brint Lland and the town for the reception and entertainment for those plying the harbour*'. Cromwell found '*the town is well seated, pretty strong, but marvellous capable of further improvement*'. In 1651, Cromwell's first cannon shot shattered the Provost's china shop and all hope of municipal resistance thereby faded!

At Rossend Castle, in 1563, the impossibly romantic great nephew of Bayard, Chastelard made his last amorous approach to Mary, Queen of Scots by secreting himself in her bedroom for the second time. For this final indiscretion he was beheaded at the Mercat Cross, St Andrews, declaiming poems by Ronsard.

64 St Columba's Parish Church, East Leven Street, 1592-5

Harled with ashlar angle buttresses, it is one of the finest 16th-century post-Reformation churches in Scotland, indicative of the town's former importance. Its squat pinnacled tower (octagonal belfry rebuilt 1749) presides majestically over a piended roof. On the east wall a forestair, 1679, leads directly to the loft thereby allowing sailors to leave the service 'to catch the tide'. The simplicity of its arched construction adds dignity to the impressive interior. Note the carved magistrates' pew, 1606, round north-east pier and early 17th-century painted panels of the mariners' loft.

65 Rossend Castle, from 1554

Strategically sited on a cliff overlooking the harbour, the original four-storey block with turnpike stair jamb was extended west in the early 17th century. Although given up for lost many times during its colourful history it enjoys a happy ending. In 1975 Hurd Rolland,

Arts in Fife

McKean

Left *Rossend Castle today.* Above *Castle and harbour in 1848*

architects, acquired the roofless hulk and sensitively converted it into their office.

66 Royal Hotel, Seaforth Place, 1807, shows Georgian sophistication. **Harbour Place** still reveals traces of the picturesque 17th/18th-century properties which used to line it, e.g. crowsteps and forestairs at **Nos 1, 2, 3** and **29** and chimney gablet at **14. Nos 16-20 Forth Place,** c.1850, built to house employees of the rail-ferry company, have been refurbished. The same treatment is long overdue on the **Forth Hotel,** 1823, William Burn (former manse converted by John Henderson to hotel for ferry passengers), now derelict but still related to

67 Burntisland Railway Station, 1847, Grainger & Miller, a symmetrical block with grand Corinthian colonnade and cornice.

68 Parsonage House, 32 East Leven Street, 1854, R C Carpenter
A good example of mullioned-and-transomed Victorian style. A stepped motif (hardly crowsteps!) is applied to gables and dormers.

Somerville Square
Amid 20th-century 'boxes' a group of contrasting 17th-century dwellings has been preserved. **30-31** (Mary Somerville's house), late 16th century, has section of main wall typically corbelled; a massive full height chimney is expressed.
69 Masonic Lodge, next door, rebuilt in the 19th century, exhibits vernacular irregularity in fenestration and has notable 17th-century inscribed panel. **Nos 28-29**, 18th century, but rebuilt, with swept dormers and **Nos 25-27**, late 16th century, complete the group with a flourish

Revd George Hay Forbes, the great Episcopalian liturgist built the Parsonage at his own expense.

Wishart

Mary Somerville's House (*above*) Somerville Square, Burntisland, was named after Mary Fairfax Somerville (1780-1872), daughter of Admiral Sir William Fairfax, one of Nelson's captains. In this building the pioneer of women's education, who was also a brilliant mathematician and astronomer, spent her childhood. She gave her name to Oxford's first college for women.

of forestairs and jettied upper floors (pediment over No 27 dated 1720).

High Street

Early records confirm that the High Street has always been a fine broad thoroughfare. The 19th century, however, saw the replacement of most 70of the older buildings. **No 71**, Star Tavern, 18th century, is a survivor – its pantiled and twin 71crowstepped gablets recall a bygone age. **No 81**, Bank House Hotel, c.1800, has delightful Georgian formality – columned entrance commands flight of steps, windows architraved and, on ground floor, corniced. **Nos 88-94**, 19th century, retain pilastered shop fronts, pedimented first-floor windows and strong cornice and eaves.

Public Library, No 102, 1906, William Williamson

A classical essay with unusual curved projecting entrance bay and swagged motifs on upper storey. **Town Hall**, 1845-6, John Henderson. With dominating steeple and Gothic detailed windows – a motif repeated on the **Burgh Chamberlain's Office** (former Post Office), 1905, sandwiched between the Town Hall and Library.

72 Royal Bank of Scotland, No 207, early 19th century

Received its neoclassical cladding c.1870, and heralds a notable 19th-century classical façade 73up to **No 249**. **Nos 265-279**, 1899, Swanston & Legge – a terminal block in dull red sandstone designed in Flemish style, wrought-ironwork on balconies supported on massive moulded brackets.

74 St Andrew's Court, 1860

Former Free Church, converted to sheltered housing in 1983 by Wheeler & Sproson with dramatic three-storey-high glazed oriel staircase.

75Nos 1-4 Broomhill Road, 1858, F T Pilkington

Intricately detailed in contrasting colours, by 'the great *fauve* of Scottish Victorian architecture'.

Kinghorn Road

Here, east of the High Street, is 19th-century residential Burntisland. A modest but elegant terrace **Nos 45-77, 85-95**, early 19th century,

Top *High Street*. Centre *Entrance to Public Library*. Above *View beyond Town Hall to Pilkington's Houses at 1-4 Broomhill Road*

double villas **Nos 103-121** Also, **Nos 128-146**
c.1830, built effectively two-storeyed but, in
accordance with superior's conditions, the
classically detailed street front is single storeyed
and outhouses are masked by screen walls.

Erskine U F Church, 1903, J B Wilson
Entrance is deeply recessed at the base of a
square tower, upstaged by attached octagonal
stair turret and surmounted by crocketed spire.
Down Lochies Road, **Seaside Cottage,** c.1840,
is a beguiling marine villa with three-bay cast-
iron columned porch on sea elevation; and
Beach Tearoom, c.1890, in yellow and red
brick and exceptional ironwork on veranda.

Top *Kinghorn Road.* Centre *Seaside
Cottage.* Bottom *Cast-iron at the Beach
Tearoom*

76 **Grange Distillery, Grange Road,** c.1805
Picturesque group, designed to suit the hillside
– **Brewer's House; West House; bonded
warehouses,** including the graceful sweep of
pantiles on the **Long Byre. Grange House,**
1680, behind fine gate piers, 1740, has been
much altered and extended. Original moulded
doorway and dated dormer.

PETTYCUR

A curved rubble pier, 1810, protects the natural
inlet known as *'Harbour under the Hill'* (the
'ferryport' recorded on most old Fife milestones).

77 **Monument,** 1886-7, Hippolyte Blanc
Design of Victorian complexity to mark the site
where Alexander III, fell to his death.

78 **Grangehill House,** late 18th century
Elegant mansion beside Kinghorn Golf Course.

Alexander III Monument marks
the spot where on a dark night in
1286 the king's horse stumbled and
he was thrown over the cliff to his
death. Thus the Golden Age when
Scotland enjoyed peace and
prosperity came to an abrupt halt.
His heir, the Maid of Norway, died
within four years leaving a nation in
turmoil and 13 claimants to the
throne, among them John Balliol
and Robert Bruce.

View over Kinghorn towards harbour

The main block is finely detailed – on each side of pedimented doorway is Venetian window (with Doric-columned mullions) set in shallow round-arched recess. Windows in matching recesses feature in pedimented flanking pavilions. A modern segmental arch in high garden wall dramatises the approach.

KINGHORN
A Royal Burgh in 1170, for a time it prospered as a ferryport and stormbound travellers packed its inns and houses.

Kinghorn Parish Church, 1774,
George Paterson
Stands beside the rubble-quayed edge of the small bay – the Kirk Harbour, 18th century. The Sailors' Aisle, 1609, survives from an earlier church. The open belltower with ogee roof, 1894, Sydney Mitchell, adds interest to the plain exterior. Fragments of a 13th-century church.

Kinghorn c.1906

Railway Viaduct, 1847
Four massive semicircular stone arches dwarf the cluster of 18th-century homes beside the harbour – **No 40 Nethergate,** Seagate House, plain with early crowstepped wing at rear, **No 38 Nethergate** and **Nos 3-7 St Clair's Entry** are picturesque with forestairs. **Nos 28-32 Nethergate,** c.1750, were sensitively restored in 1988 by the Sinclair Watt Partnership. **No 7 Cunzie Neuk,** 17th century, comfortably accommodates itself to the slope. Glorying in asymmetrical pattern of windows and doors it features a tall, shouldered wallhead chimney.

High Street is predominantly heavy, late 19th-century architecture with some lighter touches – shops at **Nos 25-29** are Ionic-columned; **No 51** has a deep wallhead course curved to form

chimney gablet; **Nos 79-87** a monstrous angled corner at end of six bays with classical relief.
Kinghorn Primary School, Baliol Street, 1986, Regional Architect
Pleasantly domestic in scale, low-pitched Italianate roof and regular window patterns in block walls. In comparison, **Old Burgh School**, Ross Place, 1829, is institutional with clock tower.

Town House, St Leonard's Place, 1826, Thomas Hamilton, has, in spite of corbelled parapet, an alien castellated Tudor style. Parts of the upper reaches of the town have been spared redevelopment, e.g. **North Overgate, Nos 6,19** and **25**, 18th century; **Kilcruick Cottage**, lintel dated 1787 and **Nos 1-3 East Gate**, 1728.

Bow Butts House, Bruce Terrace, late 18th century
Unusual garden front overpowered by a central three-storey bow-fronted tower. The Venetian windows appear to be later additions. The unusual 18th-century **doocot** has an octagonal plan with faceted roof built on a square tower (probably an icehouse) with urns at angles. **Gate piers**, 18th century, also have urn finials.

'9 **Seafield Tower**, c.1500, is built on the foreshore about 2km north of Kinghorn. Once a four-storey tower with stair jamb at south-east, 30 it is now in ruins. Nearby **Grange House**, 16th century, on the north side original block and prominent round tower with conical roof. (Not to be confused with Grange House, Burntisland.) The Victorian south front encloses door dated 1687.

Left Bow Butts House. *Top* Kinghorn Parish Church. *Centre* Hybrid doocot. *Above* Broken pediment at Kinghorn Parish Church

49

Pitteadie, drawn by McGibbon & Ross

Thomas Carlyle and his wife frequently visited the manse while her second cousin, Walter Welsh was minister at Auchtertool, 1846-79.

81**Pitteadie Castle**, late 15th century, reveals vestiges of former glory – a severe three-storey tower house with stair jamb at south-east angle surmounted by a majestic two-storey caphouse. Its amenity is enhanced by a 17th-century walled enclosure. The Renaissance-style gateway on east side is dated 1686.

82Off the A907 is the fascinating **Balmuto**, built round the original tower. *c.*1400, with 2m thick walls. The corbelled cavetto cornice is contemporary, but the battlemented parapet dates from 1797 and the caphouse 1974; 18th-century additions were removed and the rest reconstructed in 1974-84 by the Appleton Partnership.

83**North Piteadie**, 17th century, although altered, has style – pedimented dormers and doorway (1685), single-storey wings (one with attic doocot of unusual flight-hole design).

Auchtertool Parish Church, reconstructed 1833 with later additions, is disappointing; not 84so the former manse, **Candleford House**, 1812, J Gillespie Graham, a handsome Gothic Revival work which reflects the opulent style of living of 19th-century clergy. **Auchtertool House**, early 19th century, copybook Georgian, three bays square, on plan, by two storeys high, on a raised basement, Doric-columned entrance and giant pilastered corners.

Raith House

85**Raith House**, 1693-6, James Smith Bestrides the hilltop with four massive chimney heads to punctuate the skyline. Sir William Bruce is said to have been consulted regarding its design but James Smith is the name on the building accounts. The south elevation, except for the Victorian full-length balcony (as at Balcaskie), remains plain. The three central bays of the north front bear a heavily carved pediment; the many-columned porch is Victorian. James Playfair, 1785, was responsible for internal remodelling and for the outlying pavilions with quadrant links. The plasterwork of the original entrance hall and the wrought-iron balustrade at the turnpike stair are particularly noteworthy. **Stable Square**, *c.*1800, features decorative niches and impressive central archway. **Ice House**, early 19th century, is of unusual design – two storey, with game larder above, a battle-mented circle with stair tower. **Raith Tower**, early 19th century, is a derelict Gothic folly.

Kirk Wynd, Kirkcaldy c.1870

KIRKCALDY (Colour page C2)

Coastal communities develop where boats can be landed. Hence the *'sheltered cove round the East Burn'* where its harbour took shape in the 16th century, marks the origin of Kirkcaldy. By 1650, over one hundred vessels were registered. The harbour was repaired in 1663 and extended (in 1843) to include a new pier and wet dock. For

Of Kirkcaldy, Daniel Defoe was succinct: *'one street, one mile long'.*

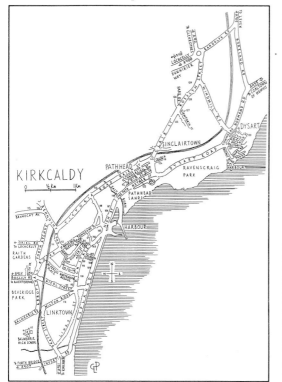

Michael Nairn in 1847 devised a form of floorcloth (i.e. cheap floor covering) by using fibre of cork and oil paint and thereby founded Kirkcaldy's famous product – linoleum which was to be its major industry for about a century. The supply of raw products, cork from Spain and whale oil from Greenland hunting grounds kept its harbour busy. Later, as whale oil became more difficult to obtain, linseed oil was used.

Old Parish Church

Wishart

Between Link Street and Sand Road (now The Esplanade) lies a disaster area for the architectural historian. The casualty list reads: **Lion's House**, *c*.1778, property of David Methven, demolished early 19th century; **Viewforth Tower**, 1790, designed by Adam brothers, demolished 1960; **Gladney**, 1711, home of William Adam, birthplace of Robert and James, demolished 1931. Gladney was a magnificent example of Scots Renaissance architecture with pedimented centre and projecting bays with curved gables.

Adam Smith, 1723-90, political economist was Kirkcaldy's most famous son. Educated at Glasgow and Oxford Universities he was appointed to the former's Chair of Logic and then of Moral Philosophy. From 1766 he lived with his mother in Kirkcaldy and in 1776 published his magnum opus *The Wealth of Nations* of which Edmund Burke fulsomely said *'in its ultimate results the most important book that has ever been written'*. It enunciated for the first time on a scientific basis the principles of political economy. Perhaps the most exciting non-academic incident in his life happened as a boy when he was kidnapped and for a short time held by gypsies in the grounds of **Strathendry Castle** where he had been staying.

the linoleum trade it was further extended in 1908. As a burgh, it was at first dependent on Dunfermline Abbey and received its Royal Charter only in 1644. Religious foundations (Abbot's Hall), Royal patronage (Ravenscraig Castle) and burgess-controlled trade were all strands which formed the original burgh. But the major impact came from the Industrial Revolution. The vicissitudes of the industry continue to have the greatest influence on the town. An industry unique to Kirkcaldy cannot be forgotten even although the scent of the 'Capital of Oilcloth' no longer permeates the air.

Today, Kirkcaldy extends along the coast, up the inland slopes, and engulfs the adjoining villages of Linktown, Pathhead, Sinclairtown, Gallatown (all annexed 1876), and Dysart (1930). After the annexations, the 'main street' (originally 1.5km long) stretched from Linktown to Gallatown, over 6km – a 'Lang Toun' indeed.

This Guide will start in the old burgh: Town Centre and the 'Back o' the Toon', and beyond; then south to Linktown and north to Pathhead, Sinclairtown, and Gallatown; finally back to the coast and on to Dysart.

86 **Old Parish Church**, Kirk Wynd
The square Norman-style tower, *c*.1500, is the town's oldest relic of the Middle Ages; loopholes suggest a defensive as well as religious role. The uncompromising box of a belfry dates from mid 18th century. The church, plain rectangular Georgian with obelisked quoins and ridge was rebuilt 1806-8 by James Elliot. In 1987, after fire damage, it was internally remodelled. At the side of the steps leading to the Church is **No 40 Kirk Wynd**, 1890, spritely Scottish Baronial, and **No 34-36 Kirk Wynd**, early 18th century, attractive vernacular with unfortunate new ground-floor windows. The popular shortcut through the Kirkyard leads to **Townsend Place**, a smart 19th-century street, particularly
87 **Nos 32-38** and **52-54. No 2 Townsend Place**, 1808, John Stevenson, as befits a Manse, is on a larger scale even discounting later additions.

88 **Fire Station**, Dunnikier Road, 1938, George Duffus
Lies to the east, its hose tower distinctively banded and roof concealed by high parapet. Certain features are reminiscent of Dunfermline Fire Station.

89**St Brycedale Church**, St Brycedale Avenue, 1877-81, James Matthews
A 60m tower and spire and associated pyramid-roofed twin towers lift the church out of the ordinary. Within its rugged rockfaced shell a transformed church at first-floor level has been provided, 1988; accesses include a lift. A multi-purpose community centre is on the ground floor.

90**Town House**, Wemyssfield, 1937-56, David Carr
Competition-winning Scandinavian-influenced design with interesting details and Nordic towerette.

Raith Walled Garden has been effectively integrated with a modern development. The pedimented **gateway**, 1786, by James Playfair; 91sundry stretches of wall; bow-ended **Raith Lodge**, c.1790, now a sub-station; and **Garden House**, 22 Raith Gardens, early 19th century, a neat building with single-storey wings.

92**Bethelfield Church**, Nicol Street, 1830-1, George Hall
Although a plain, Presbyterian preaching 'box' it is enlivened by an east gable with urn finials and symmetrical pattern of half-round, segmented door and window openings.

From a predecessor of the **Bethelfield Church** (*above*) the Revd Robert Shirra in 1778 prayed on the beach for deliverance and immediately a gale drove John Paul Jones, the American privateer who had been threating the town, back down the Firth and into the North Sea.

At the junction of Nicol Street and High Street 93are contrasting styles: **Wemyss Building**, c.1900, red sandstone with steep-pitched château-style centrepiece. Opposite, an early 19th-century plain **tenement** block is relieved by delicate mouldings at the windows.

Left Whyte House – a mansion bereft of amenity. *Top* Town Hall – civic dignity enlivened by flourishes of the Ottoman Empire. *Below* Double Dutch at 30 Whytehouse Avenue

94**Whyte House**, off Park Place, c.1790
Giant Doric pilasters unify the east front of this 95classical mansion. **No 30 Whytehouse Avenue**, early 20th century, has delightful Dutch gables and scalloped entrance.

96 Whytehouse Mansions, 1895-8, Robert Little
On the corner of Whytehouse Causeway,
exhibiting all the exuberance of Scottish
Baronial, it signals the start of the Victorian
influence on the architecture of the High Street.

RCAHMS

Top *Kirkcaldy High Street in the
19th century.* Above *McDonald's
install a Venetian blind!*

Wishart

If the 'multiple rape' at ground-floor level is
disregarded, Kirkcaldy High Street (like
Dunfermline High Street) resolves itself into a
competitive parade of the banks, past and
present. For example, William Williamson's
97 former Royal Bank of Scotland, **Nos 151-153,**
1905, with baroque open pediment and giant
pilasters, tries to upstage the swags and rosettes
98 of Peddie & Kinnear's Bank of Scotland, **No 114,**
1887, across the road. As usual the more
restrained earlier buildings have more style, e.g.
99 the elegant **Nos 148-156,** J Gillespie Graham,
with pend leading to **New Club,** *c.*1830, with
Doric-detailed entrance. Indeed, the real interest
can be found in side streets. Apart from the lone
Ionic column and façade of Old St Brycedale
Church, 1844 (now part of Marks & Spencer) the
noteworthy in **Tolbooth Street** is on the north
side. **No 11** demonstrates that modern design
need not be out of place in a traditional setting.
No 17, 18th century, is pleasantly plain (pity
100 about the modern roof tiles) but **Nos 23-25** is a
delight in rubble walls – windows formed with
starts, skewputts scrolled, two consoled
101 doorways (one dated 1785). **Nos 215-217 High
Street** , 1859, may just as well be on the Grand

Canal – arcaded windows in Venetian façade, perforated parapet above dog-toothed cornice.

102**No 221 High Street,**
1895, Sir George Washington Browne
Balustraded redstone bay successfully turns the corner with Kirk Wynd where at the **Trustee Savings Bank**, 1890, the classical verges on the baroque. **Nos 218-22** contains magnificent Ionic-columned pend and a plaque records that here at 220, Adam Smith lived with his mother from 1767 to 1776.

103**ABC Cinema**, 1905, by J T Swanson, can appropriately be described as transitional, its turrets and bays were first built to contain King's Theatre, then Opera House, then Regal 104Cinema. **No 297, Victoria House**, rebuilt 1902, and later modernised, retains much of its Edwardian charm. **Nos 333-337 High Street**, 105late 18th century, and **Nos 339-343**, dating from the 16th century, conceal interesting details behind plain tenement façades. The former has intriguing timber and plaster back outshot. The latter was re-fronted, late 17th century (gablet late 18th century), and at rear contains stair tower. In first-floor flat there is excellent 17th-century paint, plasterwork and panelling. **Nos** 106**427-431 Harbour House**, *c*.1820, enjoys inclined approach but the high central pedimented bay makes its façade top heavy. **No 439**, 18th century, is worth a passing glance but 107**Nos 443-449** must be savoured – **Sailor's Walk**, originally a pair of 17th-century houses (reconstruction 1954-9, Wheeler & Sproson), contains all quintessential vernacular elements: harl, pantiles, crowstepped gables, projecting south gable on consoled corbeltable, small deepset openings – a much photographed building.

Along the utilitarian **Esplanade**, Kirkcaldy's massive modern buildings try desperately to 108achieve human scale. **Mercat**, 1981-3, Michael Laird & Partners. The deep roof of the multi-storey carpark is punctuated by two rows of segmental dormers and the walling is subdivided by wrought-iron insets. Beyond the 109self-effacing **Swimming Pool**, *c*.1970, R Forbes Hutchison, the walls of another **car park**, said to have been conceived deliberately as a ruin, achieve spectacular irregularity.

Sir George Washington Browne
(1853-1939),Edinburgh architect, an erudite designer partial to François Ier style as revealed in his lively Public Library, George IV Bridge, Edinburgh, 1887-90.

Sailor's Walk, with detail of consoles

[110]**Oscar's**, Thistle Street, *c*.1830
(former Philp Kirkcaldy School)
Compared with these modern efforts its
exuberant classical style (under the later
commercial overlay) still expresses a unity of
form.

Back o' the Toon
Civic dignity supported by the generosity of
enlightened millowners reigns round the formal
War Memorial Gardens, with **War Memorial**,
1923, Heiton & McKay as focal point. An
[111]unexciting **Museum**, 1925, and **Library**, 1928,
complete the terraced backdrop, *'gifted by John*
[112]*Nairn, Linoleum Manufacturer'*. **Adam Smith
Centre**, Bennochy Road, 1894-9, Dunn &
Findlay, originally Adam Smith Hall and
completely reconstructed 1973 (to mark the
250th anniversary of the birth of Kirkcaldy's
renowned son) looks west across the gardens; a
complete composition in typical Victorian
[113]classical style. The **Tramways Electric Power
Station**, Victoria Road, 1901, by William
Williamson is a study in eclecticism.

Wishart

[114]**Morningside**, Bennochy Avenue,
1890-2, Robert Little
Over-ripe Baronial with all castellated
trimmings in direct contrast with austere
[115]**8 Bennochy Avenue**, 1933-4, Williamson &
Hubbard: Cubist style with wrap-round corner
windows and garden walls stuccoed to match.
On the outskirts, beyond the dominating 14-
storey tower block **Victoria Hospital**
(Dunnikier Road, *c*.1960, Regional Hospital
Board), and **Kirkcaldy High School**
(Dunnikier Way, 1958, County Architect), both
in curtain-wall style, stands

McKean

Dunnikier House Hotel

Dunnikier House, 1791-3, Alexander Laing
Now a hotel the south front of this grand

Arts in Fife

mansion maintains original pyramid massing –
a three-storey main block with central
pedimented bay (note lunette and Venetian
windows), balustraded two-storey supporting
bays, and single-storey flanking wings.

LINKTOWN
An independent Burgh of Barony from 1663
until its annexation by Kirkcaldy in 1876,
dominated by the **Linktown Railway Viaduct**,
1845-7, by Bouch & Grainger, which looms over
Tiel Burn: rock-faced masonry giving scale to
the seven massive arches.

116**West Primary School**, Milton Road,
1874-80, Sir Rowand Anderson
A splendid example of an early Board School
complete with Headmaster's and Janitor's
Houses – simple Gothic lancet windows with
steep pitched roofs throughout. Sensitive
extension, 1990, by the Regional Architect.

117**Balwearie High School**,
Balwearie Gardens, 1964 & 1972,
Fife County Architect, recalls, in some aspects,
the 1930s, with ribbon and corner windows.
Stonework insets and contrasting geometrical
shapes on roof strive to add distinction.

PATHHEAD
This Burgh of Barony dates back to the 16th
century, and c. 1600 the chief occupation was
nailmaking. An industry carefully studied by
Adam Smith, its failure to adapt to modern
methods hastened its decline. Diversification led
to home weaving then factory spinning and
weaving, and finally linoleum manufacture
became its chief occupation.

It is recorded that in 1617 James VI
on his way to Falkland Palace
climbed **The Path**. Teams of 'Thait
(type of harness) ponies' regularly
carried goods from the harbour up
this precipitous route.

Hutchison's House

Above *Dunnikier House as it was.*
Right *As it is now, known as Path House*

On **The Path**, the way up from the harbour, are two splendid examples of styles: **Hutchison's** [118]**House**, 1793, Renaissance with superb elliptical fanlight over doorway, flanked by Doric-columned Venetian windows; matching bridge [119]wing. **Path House** (restored as Nurses' Home), 1692, is vernacular L-plan with finely carved dormerheads, moulded doorway, scroll skewputts and angle sundial. Across the surrounding wasteground the only factory now [120]in sight is **Forbo-Nairn Group**, Nairn Street, 1883, by Gillespie & Scott; a well-mannered industrial design with distinctive round-headed windows three storeys high. Recently multi-storey flats have had a bad press but the three [121]15-storey **Ravens Craig** blocks, Mid Street, 1964-5, Wimpey, with vertical ribbons of glazed balconies and well-tended landscaping have a confident sparkle.

Ravens Craig

[122]**Feuars Arms**, Bogies Wynd, *c*.1890
Its red sandstone exterior is not memorable but inside are decorative tile pictures of a shepherdess and fool by Doulton, spectacular tiled bar and stained glass. **Nos 94-104 Commercial Street**, 1905-7, extended 1914, all the baroque magnificence of Fife Regional Co-operative (once the Pathhead & Sinclairtown Reform Co-operative Society). Co-operative buildings are major architectural features in the towns and villages of this part of Fife.
[123]**Pathhead Halls**, Commercial Street, 1882-4, Douglas & Sellars; a conglomerate of Scots Renaissance with a tower which bears more than a passing resemblance to Dysart Tolbooth.
[124]**Pathhead Parish Church**, Church Street,

1822-3, is a compact Gothic church with crenellated tower; harling gives lightness, but crowsteps are too low-pitched.

SINCLAIRTOWN

This village was planned, c.1750, and built around the area north of Ravenscraig Castle on the estate of the St Clairs, Lords of Sinclair and Earls of Rosslyn. Linen weaving and pottery industries waxed and waned and by the end of the 19th century the area had been the industrial of Kirkcaldy.

125 **Old Salvation Army Hall**, St Clair Street, 1909, W Dow
The simple geometry of its façade anticipates
126 some late 20th-century revivals. **Hanklymuir Factory**, 1860; this survival, amongst so many abandoned shells of factories, contains some
127 architectural refinements. **Viewforth Parish Church,** Viewforth Street, 1875-7, J F Anderson, is a pleasant design with crenellated tower, vigorously finialed.

GALLATOWN

In the 17th century Gallatown was noted mainly for nailmaking: and then home to power-loom weaving, coalmining by the end of the 18th century, then pottery by 1817.

128 **Gallatown Co-operative Society**, Rosslyn Street, 1895, reflects the Society's affluence, a series of pediments on a long frontage. On the open central pediment the carving (three tigers with shuttles in their mouths) is the heraldic device of the Apron Society.

129 **Kirkcaldy Ice Rink,** 1937, Williamson & Hubbard
Horizontal lines, ribbon of windows and vertical

Old Salvation Army Hall demonstrates its independence

Ravenscraig Castle (*overleaf*) was begun by James II and completed as a dower house for his widow, Mary of Guildres. The Royal Accounts gave many details of its construction under the direction of Magister David Boys. In the Lay of the Last Minstrel by Sir Walter Scott, Rosabelle St Clair of Rosslyn was vainly entreated:
'Then stay thee, Fair in Ravensheuch Why cross the gloomy firth today?'
In 1847 Hans Christian Andersen who described the castle as '*so picturesque and so characteristic*' found the view across '*to Edinburgh was magnificent and unforgettable*'. The steps which lead down from the Castle to the Pathhead Sands are said to be the origin of John Buchan's *The Thirty-Nine Steps*. In the same writer's *Prester John* the first chapter is set on the Pathhead Sands.

Below left *Kirkcaldy Ice Rink* Right *Lady Nairn Avenue, Kirkcaldy*

punctuation of Art Deco era; also confirms that, without regular redecoration, the style fails to weather gracefully.

Ravenscraig Castle (See colour page C2)

McKean/Beattie

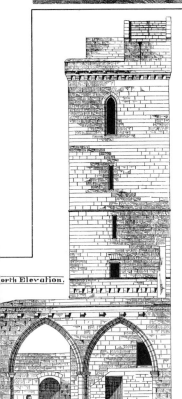

orth Elevation.

Drawing of St Serf's Tower by J Russell Walker

RIAS Library

130 Ravenscraig Castle, 1460,
David Boys, Master of Works
For over five centuries the clifftop way to Dysart has been dominated (even in its present ruined state) by this unique fortress the design of which ingeniously straddles the natural contours of the site. It is built across the neck of a narrow promontory. Consisting of two square towers, half barrelled up to 4m thick on landward (north) side, it offered stout defence against gunfire. The towers are linked by a gun platform (intended originally as hall) over a narrow entrance (served once by a drawbridge — now fixed bridge) over purpose-made ditch. It was intended that both towers would rise to the same height but in the 17th century the east tower, which descends two storeys lower than the rest of the castle, was finished off at link level leaving the west tower to reign supreme. 'Every convenience' is still much in evidence: aumbries, mural chambers, garderobes. To the south lies a small courtyard and a kitchen wing clings to the headland.

DYSART (Colour page C2)
For a century before Dysart was made a Burgh of Barony in 1510, coal was being mined there. Records confirm salt-making in 1483, and by the end of the 18th century it was making 12 million nails annually. The harbour thrived and smuggling was rife. As local industries faltered, this ancient burgh went into decline, which absorption into Kirkcaldy in 1930 failed to halt. It was the mid-20th century before its heritage

was recognised, its civic pride rekindled, and restoration of its buildings got under way. The dramatic approach to Dysart is by Sailor's Walk round the edge of Ravenscraig Park.

[31]**Dysart House**, 1755-6, now Carmelite Monastery, can be glimpsed through the trees. Once a plain symmetrical Georgian mansion with centre bow but much enlarged west and north in 1808-14 by Alexander Laing.

The main view from the park wall is across the harbour, dating from the 16th century but now a quiet backwater, to St Serf's Tower and Pan Ha'.

St Serf's Church, Shore Road, c.1500
Its great west tower immediately recalls Scotstarvit (see p.92), sombre, 22m high, ultimately relieved by corbelled parapet containing crowstepped caphouse. The most significant remnant of the church is the nave arcade.

Pan Ha' is a settlement of late 16th- and 17th-century pantiled dwellings which received the National Trust for Scotland's 'Little Houses Improvement Scheme' treatment, 1968-9, by W Schomberg Scott. Preservation, renewal and sensitive insertions created a picturesque group which, much sanitised, still recaptures a past age.

Bay House, 1 Pan Ha', dated 1583 on moulded doorway, has prominent massive chimney-breast corbelled almost at ground level. Note elaborate dormerhead and skewputts. The **Salmon Fishers' Bothy**, 1763, retains its rubble finish but the 18th-century **Girnal**, 7 Pan Ha', with chimney gablet and **Covenant House**, 8 Pan Ha', are harled. **Tide Waiter's House**, 9 Pan Ha', features a Renaissance doorway dated 1750. The **Pilot's House**, 10 Pan Ha' and **Shore Master's House**, 11 Pan Ha', complete the group. The **Anchorage**, in adjoining Wynd, 1582 (reconstructed 1965), has distinctive corbelling.

At the top of the brae, **1, 3** and **5 McDouall Stuart Place** form attractive harled and pantiled terrace. In the centre a gabled jamb with lintel, 1575, and, on Rectory Lane frontage, a curvilinear stone gablet dating from c.1700. Opposite, a small **tower block**, part of 1976 housing, Wheeler & Sproson, demonstrates that

Pan Ha' (above with the tower of St. Serf's) is the ancient name for this part of Dysart. It recalls its prosperous salt trade which gave rise to the expression *'To carry saut to Dysart'* equivalent to *'coals to Newcastle'*.

The Anchorage has been identified as 'Harbour House' in the *Day of Small Things* by O Douglas (Anna Buchan, sister of the novelist John Buchan and daughter of Revd John Buchan, Minister of Pathhead West, 1875-88).

John McDouall Stuart (1815-66) the first explorer to cross the Australian continent from south to north coast in 1861-2 was born in No 3 in the terrace which now bears his name.

Bay House – carved skewputt

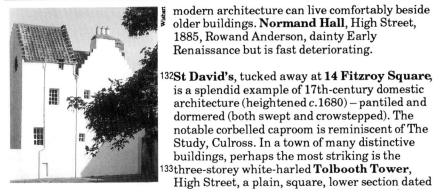

modern architecture can live comfortably beside older buildings. **Normand Hall**, High Street, 1885, Rowand Anderson, dainty Early Renaissance but is fast deteriorating.

132**St David's**, tucked away at **14 Fitzroy Square**, is a splendid example of 17th-century domestic architecture (heightened c.1680) – pantiled and dormered (both swept and crowstepped). The notable corbelled caproom is reminiscent of The Study, Culross. In a town of many distinctive buildings, perhaps the most striking is the 133three-storey white-harled **Tolbooth Tower**, High Street, a plain, square, lower section dated 1576 with interesting refinements – round stair tower, and forestair dated 1617, and octagonal bell chamber with stone ogival roof, 1707. The two-storey Victorian **municipal block** was added in 1885 by Campbell Douglas & Sellars. **Mechanics' Institute**, 1873-4, by James Aitken with arcaded ground floor and the street-gabled **58-60 High Street** complete a diverse but impressive collection of burgh architecture.

The Towers, 31 East Quality Street, 1589; restored c.1965
The four-storey stair tower unifies the composition. The harled **65 East Quality Street**, 18th century, is a counterpoint to the Georgian niceties of **69. St Serf's Church**, West Port, 1872-4, Campbell Douglas & Sellars, is competent Romanesque complete with squat broach spire recalling St Monans.

COALTOWN of WEMYSS
Built in the 1890s on Wemyss Estate for its miners. Efforts to instil some vernacular style in its 'miners rows', e.g. the harled and slated semi-detached blocks in **Plantation Row** with low links, and the crowsteps and pantiles of **Lochhead Crescent**, have earned conservation area status.

WEST WEMYSS
This Burgh of Barony since 1511 was a centre for salt-making and then, in the 19th century, a thriving coal port. The **harbour** founded by David Wemyss, c.1512, served Wemyss Castle. By the mid 20th-century it had become a 'ghost town' and only recently, since 1987, has the inner harbour been filled and the surrounding buildings restored.

Cox Stool area is picturesque in its diversity.

Top St David's. *Centre* The Towers – *16th-century romanticism. Below* Dysart Tolbooth Tower *angles a diversity of styles*

Nos 1-4 were all rebuilt in the late 19th century; 5-6 originally 'Coffee House' for visiting sailors and hence appropriately flamboyant; **7, 8-11** are severely traditional late 19th century; **12** crowstepped and **13** a 17th/18th-century merchant's house.

Cox Stool – now landlocked after harbour infill

Tolbooth, Main Street, early 18th century
A modest structure with projecting tall square bell tower and flared pyramid roof. On one side of the tower is a forestair, on the other a low pend. Most of Main Street consists of plain vernacular rows of former salters' and colliers' houses.

The shore walk west leads past the chimney-
34 gableted **Shorehead**, 18th century. **Chapel Garden**, Wemyss burial ground, against the cliff, is enclosed by walls with sculptured panels and iron gate by Sir Robert Lorimer. Nearby the

On the Tolbooth, (*below*) is a panel (now illegible) which stated '*this fabric was built by Earl David Wemyss and Town, for the cribbing of vice and service to crown*'. The cribs, or cells, were on the ground floor.

Enchantment in the Chapel Garden

Wemyss is *'one of the longest and purest of Scottish pedigrees'*. The family has been associated with this area since 12th century and acquired its name from the caves below (weems). Mary Queen of Scots first met Lord Darnley at *'The Hall of Wemyss'* in 1565. She refused *'the best-proportioned lang lad'*, but by 1566 they were married. Wemyss' primary interests were in coalmining. Sir John Wemyss owned mines at Lochgelly as early as the 13th century. To facilitate its coal trade the family developed docks at West Wemyss and Methil, built accommodation for its miners at Coaltown of Wemyss and provided Randolph Wemyss Memorial Hospital, Methil, for the care of its miners.

ruin of a superb 16th-century **house** is still recognisable; four storeys plus an attic with round central stair tower corbelled to form a rectangular caphouse. Together with **Chapel Garden House**, early 19th century, white-eaved with central chimney, they are contained within a notable 16th-century walled frontage, i.e. grilled stone arches, circular terminal towers, and central lookout.

135 **Wemyss Castle**, from 1420 (*above*)
On the clifftop, about 0.5km north-east of the village, the castle broods dramatically. A

defensive tower, c.1420, buttressed on rock with early 16th-century curtain walls north and east, it was modified and submerged as neighbours became less hostile and space became more desirable. In c.1600 a U-shaped extension used the curtain walls as outline. In 1669 the Royal Master Mason, Robert Mylne, built an L-shaped extension south. Peddie & Kinnear's Victorian accretions were removed in the 1930s by Stewart Tod and the mansion recovered much of its Restoration appearance. The 17th-century extension contains a fine panelled oak scale-and-platt staircase and excellent decorated plasterwork. **East entrance** – memorable heraldic lions and swans on gate piers, 19th century.

EAST WEMYSS
History has decreed that this village does not have the architectural merit of West Wemyss although it contains Macduff's Castle, possibly the oldest building in the area, and the **weems**, or caves, bear markings which date back to the Bronze Age. Late 19th/early 20th-century miners' rows lack appeal (as well as miners), but recent refurbishment has made **Randolph Street, St Mary's Terrace, Approach Row** and **Terrace** smart and neat. Former Wemyss Parish Church, **St Mary's by the Sea**, 1528, occupies a good site but regular rebuilding has drained it of much of its character. **Wemyss Parish Manse**, 1791, once described as 'one of the best in the country' features Venetian windows.

Top *Macduff's Castle.* Above *Reconstruction by Rosalind Taylor.* Left *Headstone by C. R. Mackintosh to Rev. A. O. Johnston, 1905, in Macduff cemetery.* Below *Miners' Row in Methil*

North along the cliffs are a series of caves – **Court Cave, Doo Cave, Jonathan's Cave, Sliding Cave** – all much desecrated but still displaying signs from the Bronze Age and Scandinavian legend, Pictish and early Christian symbols.

St Andrew's Theatre, Buckhaven

The original inhabitants of Buckhaven are said to have come from 'foreign parts' (perhaps Norway or the Netherlands); *'no more bold or skilful fishers lie at lines in the North Sea or follow the herring draive round the coast'.* In the 18th century the main occupations were fishing and weaving. In 1831 Buckhaven had 198 boats, the second largest fishing fleet in Scotland. These trades declined in the 19th century with the development of coal mines, the 'redd' from which blackened the beaches and silted up the harbour. By the mid-20th century the coal industry was dying and the harbour basins filled up.

Methil Parish Church

136Macduff's Castle, 16th century
South tower with circular stair now stands at the cliff edge like a badly decayed tooth. The rest is fragmentary although the south corner turret of the later 16th-century barmkin still exists.

BUCKHAVEN, METHIL & LEVEN
Today these three Burghs have coalesced into a continuous urban sprawl. In Old Buckhaven the houses tiered over the cliff face above the *'roaring harbour'*; these have been razed and replaced by unappealing modern housing.
St Andrew's Theatre, Church Street, has an extraordinary history. In 1869 the fisher folk bought the Episcopal Church, North Street, St Andrews, and, stone by stone, shipped it back to Buckhaven. The original church had been built in 1825 by William Burn and in 1854 Giles Gilbert Scott added an elaborate façade with finials, crockets, and buttresses. On its new site it was enlarged in 1883 and in the 1980s, under a Youth Training Scheme, the by then abandoned church, in an area of high unemployment, was transformed into a theatre.

By c.1665, Methil became a Burgh of Barony and David, 2nd Earl of Wemyss had made a harbour of its landing place. Staple industries, salt manufacture and coalmining, declined in the mid-19th century. New mines opened, the harbour, 1884-1913, underwent staged development, and Methil became the chief Scottish coal-exporting port. By the second half of the 20th century, the mines were closed and most of the infilled harbour was occupied by the constructors of rigs and other oil-related structures.

Randolph Wemyss Memorial Hospital, Wellesley Road, 1909
Built originally by the Wemyss family for the miners. Note clock turret and mini-dormers with finials.

Methil Parish Church, Wellesley Road, 1924-5, Reginald Fairlie
Stands in typical compact and resolute Romanesque style at the edge of the park open to the Firth. Arcade links the squat pyramid-roofed tower with the north transept of cruciform plan. Triple-arched motif repeated throughout. On **Cowley Street** and **Forth Street** (also visible from Wellesley Road), traditional 'Wemyss look' miners' houses have

been rehabilitated. Pantiles, crowsteps and forestairs have been retained and the entire scheme enlivened by colour washes on the harling. **White Swan Hotel**, Wellesley Road, late 19th century, has 'Jacobean' features in black and white. Closing the vista on the corner of White Rose Terrace, the five-stage clock tower with flared roof of **Tower Bar**, 1906, recalls West Wemyss Tolbooth. On monotonous **Wellesley Road**, the broad half-timbered gables at **Nos 193-277** make an interesting diversion.

In the mid-12th century, Leven comprised **Old Scoonie Church** (a fragment is now a burial enclosure), the Manse, and a few dwellings along the east side of the Leven River. By 1435, this *'Port of Markinch'* had a harbour and in 1609 achieved Burgh of Barony status. In succeeding centuries salt-panning, fishing and eventually mining thrived and then died. Today the town continues to struggle against economic adversity.

Above left *Refurbished Miners' Row in Methil*. Above *Entrance to Randolph Wemyss Memorial Hospital*

St Margaret's Queen of Scotland, Victoria Road, 1879-80, Matthews & Mackenzie Episcopal church with circular tower corbelled to octagonal belfry with spirelet, and a fine timber barrel roof and alabaster altarpiece within. Some 19th-century houses enjoy the amenity of the tree-lined grass division of **Links Road**; most are robustly Victorian, some like **Ballindalloch** with central gablet recall an earlier period. **Grey Institute, Forth Street**, 1872-4, by Andrew Heiton is sited in attractive gardens and is Gothic of unusual symmetry. **No 7 Largo Road**, 1930s, provides a rare example of Cubist style, a flat-roofed box with small box (sun room) on roof; linear emphasis by cornice, banding, glazing and railings.

'Obertal' – Largo Road, Leven

Levenmouth Swimming Pool (*left*),
1990, Regional Architect
Entertaining centre clad in Pop Art style –
banded pink blockwork with green portholes and
flume.

137**Durie House**, 1762 (*below*)
A ready-made backdrop for a Restoration
comedy, just outside the north boundary of
Leven. Seven bays wide by five bays deep and
three storeys high in restrained classical form.
The pediment over the advanced three bays
centre is urn-finialed and the tympanum is
elaborately carved. Above the Venetian-style
entrance the three windows are pedimented
(centre segmental) and all windows are

Sir Alexander Gibson, Lord
President of the Court of Session,
acquired **Durie House** (*above*) in
1614. One of the parties in a case
over which he was presiding had
him kidnapped and kept him
prisoner until the case was decided.
This episode provided the raw
material for Sir Walter Scott's
Christie's Will.

delicately architraved. The corners are visually
strengthened by rustication and the roof
minimised by peinding and platforming. In its
own way, the classical **Durie Doocot**, late 18th
century, is no less grand, 11m high octagon with
concave sides.

Leven and Ore Valleys

From Levenmouth, traditionally the east end of
Fife's industrial coastline, the River Leven runs
almost due west to its source, Loch Leven. Water
power attracted labour and spawned
communities along its banks. '*I grind the corn, I
saw the wood, I bleach the linen and I spin the
flax*'. (**The Leven**, Rankin, 1812). Apart from

Sawmill Ford, the Leven was generally unpredictable and impassible in time of flood; the first upstream crossing was **Cameron Bridge**, 17th century, reconstructed 1870. At the Meetings, about 300m west, the Leven is joined by the Ore; the source of this tributary is Loch Ore round which crowd the former mining towns of Lochgelly, Cowdenbeath, Kelty and Ballingry (all now trying to establish new identities).

THORNTON

The concrete winding towers (*below*) at **Rothes Mine** (designed to produce 5000 tons of coal per day) became the gravestones of hopes of economic regeneration as the forebodings of grey-headed miners and early suspicions of geological faults (*'frequent interruptions in the line of bearings of the coal from sea to the Lomonds'* – Statistical Account 1791-3) – proved all too true.

The first village up the Ore Valley has been a fugitive of fortune. Virtually a creation of the railway, by the end of the 19th century four lines converged on its station. Railway wagon works had been built and two hotels served its travellers. At the end of the Second World War the new Rothes pit was being sunk and the future looked prosperous. Today the station is closed, the pit long abandoned and a trunk road bypasses the village.

47 Main Street, 1897, has a four-gableted clocktower, a whimsical frontier feature.
38**Kincraig**, Peatman's Brae, 1937, is a curved-wall, flat-roof sample of the 'New Architecture'. At **10-12 Strathore Road** cottages with gableted skewputts are overshadowed by twin concrete winding towers. Almost 60m high, they formed part of the **Rothes Pithead Complex**, 1947, Egon Riss, and punctuate its elongated glazed spine. Since 1972 the towers have been used by Fife Fire Brigade.

Centre *Rothes Pit Winding Towers – headstones in an industrial graveyard*. Above *Clocktower – Main Street, Thornton*

Top *'Kincraig', Thornton*. Above
Cinema, Cardenden

The Dogton Stone, remnant of
c.10th-century Celtic cross with just
decipherable carvings fills a gap in a
dyke, about 1.5km south of
Kinglassie. From it the entire Ore
Valley can be viewed.

Coal has been mined in Fife since in
1291 a Charter granted Abbot and
Monastery of Dunfermline leave to
take coal from the lands of
Pittencrieff. Early 16th century,
Hector Boece reported *'in Fyffe are
won blackstones, quhilk has so
intolerable a heat when they are
kindallit that they resolve and meltis
irne'*. By the 18th century local
landowners – Earl of Rothes, Lord St
Clair and Earl of Leven – had
developed small estate collieries.
The change in social conditions
wrought by the upsurge of coal
mining in late 19th/early 20th
centuries is reflected in Rorie's
Mining Folk of Fife: *'Aye this is no
the place it used to be. Ye canna lie
foo at the roadside noo wi' out gettin
your pouches rippit'*. In time, the
Fife Coal Company became the
largest in Scotland. Only Longannet
remains.

KINGLASSIE
The village was developed in c.1800 for weavers
and then miners. But its mighty bings, minehead
buildings and pit-head baths have all gone. The
Parish Church, off Main Street, 1773-4,
suffered from 19th-century alterations, and its
Porch c.1700 is now roofless.

AUCHTERDERRAN
The old part of a cluster of mining villages
developed in the late 19th century; almost
obliterated by Bowhill, Cardenden, and the grey
pyramids of mine waste (now the subject of a
Land Renewal Project). The **Parish Church**,
Woodend Road, 1789, was enlarged in Gothic
style, 1890-1, by William Constable, and is now
in iron 'stays'. The 17th-century kirk beside
Derran Burn was plundered. North aisle and
early window were retained for present church.
The **Cinema**, Station Road, c.1936, *moderne*
features twin drum towers, vertical ribs, low
reliefs: now disused.

LOCHGELLY
The highest town in Fife, it sits on a ridge
between Loch Ore and Loch Gelly, once a wild,
desolate moorland inhabited by gangs of
marauding gypsies. In 1836, mineral rights were
granted. When coal mining prospered it became
a black dusty boomtown. Now that the pits are
no more its future lies to the south, to the
opencast mining at Muirhead, the East Fife
Regional Roadway, and Mossmorran
Petrochemical Complex, 1981-4 (twinkling lights
and cloudy discharges on the next ridge).

St Andrew's Church, Bank Street, 1854-5;
reconstructed in 1915 by P MacGregor Chalmers
All-embracing nave roof (punctuated by piended
dormers) extends over aisles. **Co-operative
Building**, Bank Street, 1909-10; the grandiose
front reflects the affluence of the Society. Florid
classical details continue round the corner
clocktower and along Chapel Street. **Lochgelly
Centre**, Bank Street, 1976. Multi-activities
(entertainment, leisure, art) are articulated in
utilitarian Brutalism. A deep 'frieze-like' band
struggles to give some coherence.

Lochgelly High School, Station Road,
1986-7, Regional Architect
Aggregation of inter-linked piended-roofed units.
Straight eaves over serrated plans cast subtle

Wishart

The Lochgelly Gypsies:
A plundering race
Still eager to invade
On spoil they lived
And made of theft a trade
(Houston's Parish Meeting) *The Lochgelly* was the name given to the tawse, the locally manufactured teacher's strap the use of which is now no longer permitted in schools.

Left and below *Lochgelly High School.* Below left *Shattered relic of Lochore Castle.* Bottom *Lochgelly Co-operative*

shadows. Broad horizontally banded brick and roughcast elevations succeed in this award-winning project.

Lochore Meadows Country Park, 1969-70
Reclamation from the devastation caused by the mining industry was one of the greatest operations of its kind in the United Kingdom. Today the quiet rural beauty of former times has been restored. The largest loch in Fife

Mary Pit – Winding Tower

In 1825, Sir Walter Scott's son married **Jane Jobson**, niece of Sir Adam and Lady Fergusson and heiress to part of old Lochore estate. The writer often visited the district and Ballingry Church is mentioned in *The Abbot*.

It is not all coal in Cowdenbeath. In the district, prehistoric settlements have been identified and the site at Beath Kirk has been used for Christian worship since the 13th century. Locals are keen to point out that during Queen Victoria's only visit to Fife in 1842, she actually passed through the town

(approximately 125 hectares) has been created. At Park entrance stands an immense **pit-winding wheel**. Nearby, the ruin of **Lochore Castle**, 14th-century Norman style keep within 12th-century barmkin wall. **Park Centre**, *c.*1970, contemporary and discreet; north-east, the gaunt frame of the winding tower of **Mary Pit**, 1902, sole relic of the district's six mines.

BALLINGRY
This is one of Scotland's oldest parishes but little remains of the village which was engulfed in the late 19th century by the miners' rows of Lochore, Crosshill and Glencraig.

Parish Church, Ballingry Road, 1831, Ebenezer Burrell, incorporates belfry and interesting classical window on the north gable, 1661, from 17th-century church.

[139]**Lochore House**, *c.*1790, is a boarded-up gem on the south slope of Benarty foothills. Venetian doorway and window is set in fine ashlar [140]masonry edged with rusticated quoins. **Benarty House**, *c.*1830, William Briggs, 1.5km west, is more pretentious. Ionic-porticoed main block linked by convex quadrant walls to pedimented pavilions. Its **steading**, *c.*1840, observes the classical courtyard layout.

Cowdenbeath Municipal Buildings

COWDENBEATH

In the period 1850 to 1914, the population grew from 1000 to 25,000 and it earned the sobriquet 'Chicago of Fife'. Once the metropolis of the Fife Coal Fields it accepted as an occupational hazard its description *'where the buildings sink and lean'.*

141**Beath Church**, Old Perth Road, 1834-5, by James Macfarlane, sits on a ridge. Replacement of 1640 church – plain elevations with hood-moulded windows. The **Kirkyard**, which received the attention of Burke & Hare, has gravestones dating from the 18th century.

Town House, High Street,
1904-6, T Hyslop-Ure
Municipal style going 'over the top' to impress; even dumpy clock tower, columned, pedimented and domed. High Street hostelries compete in artisan classical: **Commercial Hotel**, late 19th century, and **Gothenburg House**, 1895. **Social Club** (former cinema), High Street, early 20th century, reflects the Art Deco influence. Severe rectangular composition (flanked by slightly recessed single-storey wings) is relieved only by a band of Greek key motif. **Miners' Institute**, Broad Street, 1925, J T Scobie, has an institutional, classical style which now looks weary whereas the domestic scaled **Broad Street Centre for the Handicapped**, late 20th century, bristles with confidence.

Timber Housing, Main Street, Lumphinnans, was probably an attempt to counter the *'sink and lean'* problem. Log-finish, piended dormers, projecting barges and eaves seem more appropriate to the Forestry Commission than to the Fife Coal Field.

KENNOWAY

Its fortune waned when the traffic from Pettycur to Tayport changed to the New Inn route. But the new main road, c.1800, and the development of the weaving and shoe-making industries led to an upturn during the 19th century.

Parish Church, Cupar Road,
1849-50, Thomas Hamilton
Romanesque Revival with distinctive square-shouldered gables to contain the flat-roofed galleried aisles. The slim tower with broach spire looks an afterthought. **Cockburn House**, Cupar Road, c.1800, displays a rich classical

Windygates
Immediately north of Cameron Bridge is the once bustling posting station of Windygates where changes to Pettycur, and hence by ferry to Edinburgh, could be obtained. At the central road junction is the black and white **Windygates Hotel**, early 19th century.

Kennoway Parish Church

Kennoway enjoyed early prosperity from malting and brewing. The 1793 Statistical Account recalls that in 1753 the traffic from Pettycur to Tayport ferries passed up the Causeway.

Rob Roy MacGregor set spoil to the castle in 1716 foraging in Fife after the Battle of Sheriffmuir. MacGregor surprised a party of about 100 Swiss mercenaries near Cameron Brig and his men exploded a barrel of gunpowder under the postern-gate to try to render the castle indefensible.

vocabulary, with rusticated end pilasters with rosettes, and fluting at frieze.

Causeway

This old main street retains some of its original character as it makes its irregular climb north past the Old Kirkyard. At north end it is not too late to restore crowstepped **Lodge St Kenneth**, early 18th century. By comparison, the early 19th-century **Fernbank**, with high-walled garden beside the Old Kirkyard, looks in excellent 142 shape. To the west of the village **Kingsdale House**, late 18th century – large extensions, 1804, into substantial mansion classically 143 garbed. **Newton Hall**, 1824, David Bryce, Jacobean including diagonal shafted chimneys.

Newton Hall

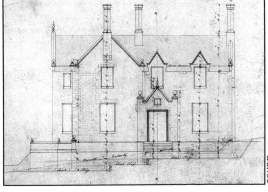

RCAHMS

Below right *88-90 Main Street, Coaltown of Balgonie.* Below *Balgonie Castle courtyard drawn by McGibbon & Ross*

McKean

Coaltown of Balgonie, mining village dating from the late 18th century. **88-90 Main Street**, early 19th century, with classical touches.

Wishart

144**Balgonie Castle**, from 15th century
A fine example of a tower house later extended into a palace. The site is just over 1.5km south-east of Markinch on the south bank of the river

RCAHMS

Leven. The bleak, 20m high tower (with walled courtyard) dates from early 15th century (gabled attic is 16th century). Daughter of Sir John Sibbald, owner of property late 14th century, married Sir Andrew Lundy who built 1469 addition – two-storey range now forms north side of courtyard. In 1706 the 3rd Earl of Leven erected the three-storey range which replaced a screen wall linking the north range to the 17th-century two-storey house in the south-east angle of the enclosure. Damage in 1716 during the occupation of Rob Roy MacGregor, and later deterioration due to neglect, was arrested when restoration of tower began in 1978 by Cunningham, Jack, Fisher & Purdom.

The most illustrious owner of Balgonie Castle (*above*) was **General Sir Alexander Leslie** (acquired in 1635) – a Covenanting officer who served with distinction under Gustavus Adolphus in the Thirty Years' War and rose to the rank of Field Marshal in the Swedish army. In 1641 he was created 1st Earl of Leven and Lord Balgonie. He retired in 1654 and undertook the reconstruction of the north range and laid out extensive gardens. He was buried 'in his own iyle' in Markinch Church in 1661. Early in the 18th century Defoe commented 'the situation very pleasant. The park is large, but not well planted; at least the trees do not thrive'.

MARKINCH
Some claim that Markinch was the capital of Fife when Fife was one of the seven provinces of Pictland. Others claim that the terraces on Markinch Hill denote a Roman camp. All are agreed that the church succeeded a 6th-century preaching station of St Drostan, nephew of St Columba.

Parish Church, Kirk Brae, 1786, rebuilt by Thomas Barclay
Enlarged in stages during the 19th century. But the tower, *c*.1200, dominates the town – and bears a striking resemblance to St Regulus, St Andrews (see p.118). Earlier pyramid spire was

Above Window of Session House.
Right Markinch Parish Church

replaced by octagonal version on stepped base in 1807.

Session House, 1875, Rowand Anderson Incorporated fragments of medieval carving at west gable window. Old maps confirm that 18th- and 19th-century houses nestled round the hillock of the church. Hence **Kirkstyle**, 13 Kirk Street, early 19th century, has scrolled skewputts – a distinctive feature of these older houses. The two levels at **9-11 Kirk Street** have been successfully married. **Galloway Inn**, Kirk Street, late 18th/early 19th century, an old coaching inn before advent of railways, retains its pilastered entrance. **No 11-11a School Street**, 1800-1, Neil Ballingal; extended 1825, Robert Hutchison. East part originally school.

Commercial Street contains a variety of interesting buildings; **41-43** and **33-35**, early 19th century, have trim piended dormers; **42**, late 18th century, was obviously thatched, now pantiled. At corner of **Cubbs Close** is a neatly contrived curved chimney gablet with circular attic window amidst the embellishments. **2-10 Croft Row**, an early 19th-century terrace, offsets double-splayed corner frontage of **Well Park**, 1895, where good mouldings integrate shop and house. **Radnor, 20 Commercial Street**, early 19th century, is excellent late-Georgian with fluted frieze and upper columns.

Markinch Railway Station (including Station Master's House), 1847, Thomas Grainger Tudor Italianate style was perhaps suggested by

Radnor, Markinch

the conventional roofs for platforms – low-pitched, projecting and supplies just enough classical detail to endow a practical solution with character.

Balbirnie Estate
This historic estate, dating from c.1312, once had three seams of workable coal. Happily it is now becoming a recreational centre for the surrounding area, for all to enjoy.

Stob Cross, high on the bank beside East Lodge of Balbirnie House, is said to mark the limits of Sanctuary of Markinch Church.

Balbirnie House

Arts in Fife

145 Balbirnie House, from 17th century
Now a hotel, this ancient mansion was clothed with fashionable classical front block in 1777-82 by John Baxter jun. His south-west front formed a seven-bay block on raised basement with centre advanced and pedimented. The next substantial addition, 1815-19, proved a testing exercise in architectural composition for Richard Crichton whereby Baxter's frontage became the north-west end of the new frontage; matching sections were added on the south-east. The cornice from the projections is now carried on Ionic columns straight across a new central recessed section. The arched forms flanked by pilasters are reflected in the new attic accommodation and a new extended south-east front includes the entrance (marked by impressive Ionic portico). The resultant Greek classical mansion is massive yet elegant and has been favourably compared with Camperdown House, Dundee, c.1824, William Burn. In 1989, it was converted to a hotel. The **Stable Block**, c.1780 (imaginatively adapted, 1972-3, for craft workshops), is a vernacular quadrangle with pediment over round-arched entry. The **South Lodge**, 1861, David Bryce, exudes Victorianism.

The historic route across Fife to the low col between East Lomond and Clatto Ridge was marked by excellent stone bridges over the River Ore and Lochty Burn and, at first, a ford (still discernible) over the River Leven. Later, in 1710, a bridge was built, to be replaced by the present Balbirnie Bridge, c.1792. Nearby once stood (now only some outbuildings remain) 'The Plaisterers – a very convenient inn built by Thomas Alburn, an Englishman and the best plaisterer that ever there was in Scotland'. (Lord Balfour, 1725). He doubtless worked on Leslie House. In the Second Statistical Account the Revd Andrew Murray referred to his report of 1790 regarding a projected turnpike road 'to have run from the Plaisterers' Inn on the Leven to the Kirk of Beath. It was to give a shorter and better time of travelling towards St Andrews, Dundee and Cupar on the one hand, and towards Queensferry, Dunfermline, Edinburgh and Glasgow on the other'. It would seem that exactly 200 years later the turnpike road has appeared as the East Fife Regional Road.

The **Edinburgh & Northern Railway** also followed the historic route to central Fife and in 1847 the **Markinch Railway Viaduct** was built by Thomas Grainger *'a splendid viaduct of ten arches about seventy feet in height which form a striking object in the scene'*. (Tullis). The proposed direct rail branch line from Markinch to Leslie was *'opposed by Lord Rothes on the grounds that it would be injurious to his policies'*. Hence the final circuitous route necessitated two spannings of the Leven valley – the **Balbirnie Viaduct** (1861), 10 semicircular rubble arches, and the graceful 14-arched **Cabbagehall Viaduct** (1861), at Leslie.

Below Leslie House. Bottom The Bull Stone, Leslie Green

West Lodge, R & R Dickson, with its columned porch, reflects the style of the mansion. Hurd Rolland's **Club House** for Balbirnie Golf Club has nicely detailed brick service core supporting all-glazed, upper floor with balcony.

¹⁴⁶**Leslie House**, 1667-74, John Mylne jun. and son Robert (it is said that Sir William Bruce was 'consultant')
Only the west range survives of original quadrangular building built on terraced north bank of the Leven. Described by Defoe as the *'Glory of Fife'*, it was unfortunately burnt down in 1763. The west front, reconstructed 1765-7, became a typical classical composition. The 19th century saw the introduction of balustraded parapet and additional dormers. Sir Robert Lorimer, 1906-7, titivated the west front and

Arts in Fife

remodelled the south gable. The vaulted ground floor of the original north range remains. A rock garden has been devised in the foundations of the south range. It is now an Eventide Home. The original magnificent **gate piers**, late 17th century (resited late 18th century), can be found beside the Baronial **Duke's Lodge**, 1906.

LESLIE

The Burgh of Barony, 1458, developed along a ridge sheltered on the north by the Lomonds. It was spared industrial disfiguration as the late 18th-century mills were built to the south, in the valley of the River Leven. As a result, Leslie Green can easily be regarded as the centre of a

Wishart

quiet rural community, especially as the ancient **Bull Stone** is a relic of country fair entertainment.

Top *Christ's Kirk on the Green, Leslie.* Centre *37-51 Glenwood Road, Leslie.* Bottom *80-102 High Street, Leslie*

Christ's Kirk on the Green, Greenside Rebuild 1868-9, by Alexander Leslie of Barclay's 1819-21 church which replaced the original Kirk on the Green. A simple Gothic Revival building. Its pyramidal roofed tower with corner gargoyles supplies much-needed authority. The featureless Rothes and Douglas Vaults are said to be the 17th-century aisles of the early church.

Nos 1-16 Greenside, c.1800, a pleasing terrace punctuated by chimney gablets with windows. Pends offer tantalising glimpses of Lomond Hills. Once again, the oldest part of the town (east end of High Street) is nearest the church – **Nos 15-19** and **50-52** date from the 18th century, the impressive **Nos 80-102** from the 17th. The 1854 Town Plan clearly indicates the contrast between the gentle medieval curve of the Old Town High Street and the straight lines of the New Town section. At the west end, the 19th-century **Mansefield**, supported by single-storey wings, maintains its dignity surrounded by a nursery garden. Note fascinating stone-canopied terrace, **Nos 37-51 Glenwood Road**, 19th century, built for flax spinners.

47**Strathendry Tower**, c.1600, is a severe tower, with corbelled bartizan on east gable, which time has slowly domesticated, i.e. windows enlarged, swept wallhead dormers introduced

The artificial course from Loch Leven to Auchmuir Bridge, known as New Cut, 1832, guaranteed all mills (of which at one time or another there were around 25 in all) a more regular and plentiful flow of water.

The earliest known stone house in Glenrothes is the ruin of 17th-century Pitcairn House, Leslie. It is the remains of a two-storey house belonging to a Jacobite physician, *a good new house with enclosure belonging to the learned Archibald Pitcairn, MD, a Cadet of Forther'* (excavated in 1980 by Glenrothes Development Corporation).

The initial population target in 1948 was 32,000. By 1963, in order to offset the Rothes mine failure and attract diverse industries, it was raised to 55,000 with the possibility of 70-95,000 by the end of the 20th century. The original aim of the planners *'to establish a self-contained and balanced community for working and living'* has never been forgotten.

Typical detached dwelling, Glenrothes

Glenrothes' site has a long history. Radiocarbon-dating indicates 3000 BC as the construction date of Balfarg Henge, within which grave pits and artefacts have been found. The Balbirnie Stone Circle, c.2000 BC, a small example of *'the cathedrals of prehistoric Scotland* and known locally as the 'Druids' Circle', was excavated and relocated to facilitate road-widening in 1971 near North Lodge.

and tight defensive stair replaced by stair tower in 1699. Sympathetic office ranges by William Burn, 1824, and David Bryce, 1845.
Strathendry House, 1824, by William Burn, exhibits his penchant for Jacobean revival. Curvilinear gable on central east bay window and hood mouldings extend into strong string-courses.

148**Water Treatment Works**, Lomond Hills, 1988, Regional Architect
Follows recent Italianate trends in official architecture; the administration block has the convent look.

GLENROTHES

This is a New Town (not grafted on to any other) occupying an area of great natural beauty astride the River Leven between Markinch and Leslie. Blessed with ample space its planners followed Garden City principles of well-landscaped, low-rise, suburban layouts with excellent inter-linking roads and generous 149parking areas. (**Raeburn Heights**, 1968, remains the only venture into high-rise flats). Regrettably, growth has not followed the Fife tradition around the kirk, tolbooth and market 150place. Instead there are the **Kingdom Shopping Centre**, started 1961, Peter Tinto and massively enlarged at regular intervals; the interior is lively, the exterior is dull and confused by loading and parking facilities; and 151**Fife Regional Headquarters** (extension), North Street, 1989, Regional Architect, a striking lightweight contrast to the existing heavy, spec-built, concrete offices; south façade embellished by a town clock, as a civic focal point, has a certain Scottish verticality in design, albeit in brick and glass.

Glenrothes presents a fascinating cavalcade of architecture typical of the second half of the 20th century. Early 1950s housing in **Bighty** and **Carleton Avenue, Woodside**, is traditional, harled, with steep-pitched roofs and dormer windows. Later four-storey Y-plan blocks at **Queen Margaret Drive, Auchmuty**, add variety. Assorted mono-pitches on the braes at **Cadham** reflect the inclinations of the 1980s.

The style of shopping centres also reflects 152changing fashion. **Woodside**, 1954, derived from Harlow New Town, is in rectangular blocks with balcony access to houses above shops, whereas the most recent is the attractive centre at 153 **Cadham**. Good brickwork is overshadowed by

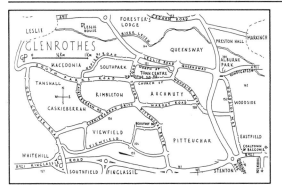

low-pitched, piended roofs (note the interesting fenestration at the **Ring o' Stanes Inn**). The style is infectious e.g. **North Glenrothes Neighbourhood Centre, Small Workshop Units** (off Pitcoudie Avenue), and **Huntsman's House**, HQ for Corporation Technical Services. On the higher ground, **Sheltered Housing Complex** repeats similar roofs at various levels, also on a squat campanile. Turn-of-the-century-style wrought-iron gates and fences are thoughtful accessories.

Centre left *Ring o' Stanes Inn*. Left *Fife Institute of Physical and Recreational Education.* Top *Fife House.* Above *Viaduct near Leslie*

154 The swimming pool of the **Fife Institute of Physical & Recreational Education**, Stenton Road, 1970, sports patterned glazing, and a bold 155 brise-soleil. Across Viewfield, **Crystals Arena** escapes industrial labelling with sculpted effect of vertical cladding.

Industry being Glenrothes' life-blood, factories appear in all shapes and sizes, mostly utilitarian. Some exploit modern technology, e.g. 156 **Saltire Centre Advanced Units**, Viewfield – neat, effectively giant portakabins; at Southfield 157 the **Kineticon** 'tilt-up' factory and the classic simplicity of the wall panels at **PAC-Systems**.

158 The dramatic sculpture effect of **St Paul's Church**, Warout Road, 1956-7, by Gillespie Kidd & Coia, and Benno Schotz's *Crucifix and Our Lady's Piece* touch a deep chord.

159 Later protective cladding on **St Columba's Church**, Church Street, 1960-1, Wheeler & Sproson, emphasises its box-look, diminishing the religious concept.

160 **Glenrothes Area Social Work Office**, South Street, 1990, Fife Regional Architect Symmetry in brick. A crisp colourful building it is both civic and inviting. One of the most 161 successful buildings is the **Leonard Cheshire Home, Pitteuchar**, 1983-5, Wheeler & Sproson, which also repeats the roof-dominated brick formula. Schools record a complete range of 162 stylistic change from the long, low **Carleton Primary School**, Happer Crescent, 1951, Fife 163 County Architect, to the **High School**, Napier Road, 1966-7, Fife County Architect, whose curtain-walled blocks surround its impressive, elevated, bowed assembly-hall wing.

The town boasts colourful signs at entries to industrial estates, and its sculptures are noteworthy, e.g. the witty parade of the sculpted 164 **Hippos**, 1972, Stanley Bonnar; *Seated Old Couple* in the Shopping Centre, 1979, by Malcolm Robertson, and outside the Bus Station, Benno Schotz's inspiring *Ex Terra*, 1965.

165 **Stenton Community Centre**, Dunrobin Road, 1978, is an imaginative re-use of a farm steading. 19th-century **Balfarg Steading** is being rehabilitated as a theatre and centre for the arts. **Alburne Park**, Levenbank (19th century), retains wallhead gable and hood moulds. This well-established area on the south bank of the Leven has some modern private 166 houses, e.g. **Casa Villa,** No 6 Orchard Grove.

Top *'Ex Terra' – literally!* Above *Advance factory units, Saltire Centre*

When told by the **priest of St Paul's** that his people were asking him why the cross was not centred on front, the architect, **Jack Coia**, never at a loss for words, replied *'Tell them any goddam fool could have put it in the middle'*. (Rogerson's biography, 1986)

Top *St Paul's RC Church*. Left *PAC-Systems*. Above *Marching Hippos*. Below *Leonard Cheshire Home, Pitteuchar*

Howe of Fife – view towards West Lomond

Eden Valley (south)

West of Cupar the rich agricultural valley of the Eden is known as the Howe of Fife. Once this area was covered by thick forests, bogs and even a loch (Rossie). Historically, therefore, it is logical to treat the south and north banks of the Eden separately. This section starts on the route round the shoulder of the West Lomond. Many Scottish kings and queens followed this track as they made for their hunting lodge at Falkland.

Falkland's Royal visitor list is impressive. James I acquired it by 'compulsory purchase' from the Earl of Fife and James I, II and III extended it and spent long periods in residence. James IV entertained the English pretender Perkin Warbeck at Falkland in 1495. James V as a youth knew it as a prisoner under the Earl of Angus but returned to carry out massive reconstruction in 1525-42. It was here, on his deathbed, that he learned his wife had given birth to a daughter and he gave vent to his feelings 'It cam wi' a lass, and will gang wi' a lass'. He proved unduly pessimistic. The Stewart line endured until 1714 with the death of Queen Anne.

The fame of **Falkland's Forest** is recognised in the Burgh seal – a stag crouching under a tree. All the visiting Royalty including Mary Queen of Scots hunted in the forest. The security it offered to royalists and the raw material it provided for defence prompted Cromwell to order its clearance in 1652. He incidentally used the timber to fortify Perth.

The Loch of Rossie encroached on the Parish of Auchtermuchty where, in 1531, a Charter for its fishing rights was issued. The Loch was finally drained in 1805.

167**Pittillock House**, 16th/17th century, an L-plan tower house, had a classical facelift in the mid-19th century resulting in an expansive east front, three storeys of five bays edged with margins.

168On hillside, **Chapelyard House**, early 19th century, is a comely two-storey supported by single-storey wings.

FALKLAND

In the 14th century, Macduff's castle ruled from this strategic site, where the north/south Fife route crossed the Eden Valley. Foundations of the castle can still be traced in the grounds of the Palace. The town received its Royal Charter in 1458 and, with the commercial rights, was able to support the Royal Court, who came to hunt in the ancient forest.

After the Union of the Crowns Royal patronage waned but the hand-loom weavers prospered (800 are recorded by the mid-19th century). At the end of the 19th century power-loom factories had been established and were to endure well into this century. Architecturally the burgh is of enormous interest. Like Culross, it was spared much of the 19th-century 'improvement' but in Falkland many houses are more than 300 years old. They had been thatched, later replaced with pantiles, imported in the 17th century and, in the 18th century, home-made at nearby

Falkland was, it is claimed, James VI's favourite palace and Mary Queen of Scots who loved hunting in its forests was a frequent visitor. Mary of Guildres ordered a new coalhouse *'domus pro carbonibus'* and the Duke of Rothesay was allegedly murdered there. Charles I continued its Royal patronage and it was at Falkland that Charles II first constituted the Scots Guards. Today there is a Hereditary Constable, Captain and Keeper for Her Majesty the Queen, and the National Trust for Scotland are Heritable Deputy Keepers.

Left *Entrance to Falkland Palace – trés formidable!* Below *'A cat can look at a king!'*

Dunshelt. The burgh layout is typically medieval: the main street with east and west ports, a parallel minor street and narrow cross wynds.

Falkland Palace, 1500-13, 1537-41
A cluster of gems; difficult to categorise. Some say it is Gothic/Baronial/Palladian, others say Franco-Scottish with Italianate overtones. Today it is a three-sided quadrangular structure varying from mere foundations, in the north range (burnt by Cromwell's troops, 1654), to a fully operational south range.

At the west end of the south range is the three-storey gatehouse, 1539-41. Like the Palace of Holyroodhouse, the pend entrance is squeezed between massive round towers, crenellated with conical roofs *(prik ruiffis)*.

The rest of the south range, 1511-13, is a fusion of styles. On the street frontage vertical

Courtyard façade of the Palace drawn c.1847 by R. W. Billings

Gothic blends with Renaissance. Niched buttresses intersect string-courses and elaborately corbelled parapet. The courtyard façade of the lean-to corridor, refaced in 1537-42, has finely detailed buttresses of Corinthian columns. In each bay two roundels were carved by French masons. The roof is alternately punctuated by lofty classically coped chimneys and segmentally pedimented dormers. The ground-floor accommodation is vaulted. The first floor has habitable rooms, the second floor contains the Chapel – a stately chamber with oak ceiling, c.1540, painted 1633, and timber screen c.1540. The turnpike stair in squat tower at the east end has a great hollow newel.

Of the east range only the wall of the courtyard façade, c.1510 (which generally matches that of the south range), remains. There is matching turnpike tower at the north end and some vaulted cellarage. On its east side (originally a projection now like a tower house with its own guardroom, postern and turnpike tower), is **Croce House**, 1529-32, where 19th-century rebuilding has restored the King's Bed Chamber.

Stable Block, 1528-31, unadorned western elevation with slit windows. **Caichpule**, 1540-1 (restored c.1890) – an enclosed court attached to stable block where Royalty indulged in an early form of tennis.

Tornaveen, High Street, a late Victorian curiosity with sculpture attributed to James Galloway. **Moncreif House**, High Street, 1610 is the only remaining thatched roof in Falkland. Openings are roll-moulded with small classical touches. Inscribed panel expresses (at length) loyal greetings from Nicoll Moncreif, 'King's Averiman'. **Hunting Lodge Hotel**, High Street, 1607, has an additional storey and remodelling included artisan doorways in 19th century. Mouldings at first-floor windows are original. Another panel with loyal sentiments. **Town Hall**, High Street, 1800, Thomas Barclay, is a pre-Baronial triumph. In spite of vernacular surroundings and contrast with the twin-towered Palace entrance its plain classical style has a self-contained dignity. The square clock tower, octagonal belfry drum, and faceted spire are nicely proportioned.

At this point the High Street broadens into The Cross at the centre of which is the garishly painted **Bruce Fountain**, in Victorian Gothic, 1856, A Roos. **Covenanter Hotel**, 1771, is embellished with Doric columns and swagged frieze; east extension is unashamedly Baronial. The outstanding building in the tall terrace at the south-west corner of The Cross is **Cameron House**, early 17th century, with late 19th-century regular fenestration within vermiculated quoins.

Old Town House, 1866, on the west side of The Cross, is in Baronial garb, incorporating earlier relics. **Fountain House**, The Cross, 1735, was later remodelled. Note grotesque on skewputt. **Parish Church**, The Cross, 1848-50, David Bryce, is well-buttressed, tower being double buttressed at each pinnacled angle. Original pews convert to communion tables.

On the north side of the High Street is an architectural sandwich: the **Saddlers**, 1771, and **St Andrew House**, mid-18th century (dormers, 19th century), reflect douce native architecture. In the middle, the **Gift Shop** (former Post Office), early 19th century, is blatantly Gothic with timid battlements.

The secondary medieval street, now Horsemarket and Brunton Street, is full of interest. On **Horsemarket**, at South Street corner, the **Fruit Basket**, c.1800, has slim Doric at entrance and round stair tower at back. On corner of Back Wynd, **House**, c.1700, retains its

Richard Cameron, 'Lion of the Covenant' was born at Cameron House, Falkland, in 1648. Educated at St Andrews University, 1662-5, he was 'converted by the field preachers'. With a price on his head he evaded capture until, after a brave fight, he was killed at the Battle of Aird's Moss in 1680 by Bruce of Earlshall who took his head and hands to Edinburgh.

The Co-operative Factory at Falkland moved George Scott-Moncrieff to generalise, somewhat unjustly (on all parties) 'Co-operative architecture in Scotland merits any abuse that may be levelled against it; it combines all the dignity of fish-and-chip saloons with the popular appeal of bank buildings'.

Above *Moncrief House and Hunting Lodge Hotel with detail of façade of Moncrief House*

Falkland

Wishart

forestair. **Dundrennan**, 1694, boasts Victorian oriels. **Brunton House**, Brunton Street, 1712 (restored 1894-5, and 1970-1, R W Schultz), a three-storey masterpiece in rubble, pantiles and crowsteps, originally belonged to the Hereditary Falconers to the Crown. **Wester Brunton**, early 18th century, is attractively restored.

Humouring to the irregularities of the site is a feature of traditional building. For example, at the corner of High Street and Mill Wynd the picturesque **Stag Inn**, 1680, adapted at a later date to sloping corner site; the gusset **Block**, early 19th century, at corner of Brunton and High Streets, fitted to shape and levels; the natural rock foundations exposed on several properties on the north side of High Street West. **Bruce's Building**, High Street, 1869, has pulled out all the Baronial stops: nearby is a variety of forestairs. Towards West Port Victorianism predominates: e.g. 19th-century **Lomond Cottage** and **Lilac Bank Cottage**. Some older houses remain, e.g. **Embo**, and **Hollyben**, 1752, with classical entrance, and the **Weaver's Cottage**, sensitively formed out of two 18th-century cottages. **2-6 Royal Terrace**, mid 19th century, are pleasant cottages; **No 1** has neat little dormers and gablet.

William Burn (1789-1870) and David Bryce (1803-76)
William Burn, architect, was born in Edinburgh and trained under Smirke in London. In 1812 he set up what was to become a highly successful practice in Edinburgh. By the early 1820s he was acknowledged as one of the most able exponents of country house design in Britain, an expert in economical planning and in reconciling clients' conflicting requirements. David Bryce, his Chief Clerk in 1829, became his partner in 1841 and, after Burn went to London in 1844, practised on his own account from 1850. Throughout Britain, Burn was responsible for designing or radically reconstructing some 200 mansions while, in Scotland, Bryce had over 100 country house commissions. Burn started in almost a Tudor style and graduated to Jacobethan. Bryce developed the fierce neo-Baronial characteristics which were to be the hallmarks of High Victorian architecture in Scotland.

169 House of Falkland, 1839-44, William Burn
This mansion sits on a plateau between Maspie and Mill Burns with the Lomond Hills as a backdrop. It is a good example of Burn's expertise in domestic planning presented in English Jacobean with a sprinkling of Scottish detail. Externally, the main features are the mullioned parapeted main block, the square pepperpot angle turrets and the twist-shafted chimneys. The Late Victorian interior, particularly the chimneypieces and plasterwork designed by R W Schultz, is impressive.

NEWTON of FALKLAND
Hamlet dating from 18th century, once dependent on Maltings. **Bonthrone Maltings**, late 19th century, is now disused; a sprawling industrial complex with distinctive skyline of pyramid-roofs. **Balreavie Cottage**, 1735 (former school, and, before that, a brewery), presides over open space, unobtrusively supported by 18th/19th-century **Balerno** and adjacent **cottage.**

FREUCHIE
An 18th-century village of hand-loom weavers, transformed when Linen Mill was built c.1870. For those at Royal Court at Falkland, Freuchie

Above and left *House of Falkland*

was like Coventry: 'Awa to Freuchie where the Froggies live'. The **Lumsden Memorial Hall**, High Street, 1883, in assertive Victorian style, ensures that the founder of Linen Mill is not forgotten.

Linen Mill, Eden Valley Row
Unobtrusive symmetrical block, 16 bays long, including two arched cart entries: now warehouse. **Lomond Hills Hotel**, High Street, centre dated 1753. Modern swept dormers respect tradition. In west part of High Street, **West End**, early 19th century, is plain with classical touches. **Moriston**, c.1800, and **In A Nook**, 1769, retain some vernacular features.

Top *Linen Mill, Freuchie*. Above *'Lathrisk'*

Kettlebridge was a 19th-century hamlet of weavers whose terraced houses, much improved, still exist. The 1831 bridge with 'dippen steps' links Mid and North Streets.

Kettle Parish Church

170**Lathrisk**, c.1740, reconstructed 1786
Fine sequestered mansion on the alluvial plain by the River Eden. Early house is linked by stair bay to classical block with seven-bay east front with Venetian doorway. Venetian-windowed pavilions are extended by quadrant walls and gatepiers to complete a dramatic façade.
Laundry Block (now house), late 18th century, is emphatically Gothic including Y-tracery. Stylish **Home Farm House**, 1852, features restrained classical detailing throughout.

KINGSKETTLE
Another community developed round weaving but now land and dormitory oriented.

Kettle Parish Church, 1832, George Angus, Tudor Gothic, with a five-stage tower seen throughout the parish and beyond; pinnacled octagons support its latticed parapets.
Canmore, Corn House, Kerr Cottages and **14 Main Street**, all dating from 18th century, sympathetically restored, irregularly combine to form the most picturesque group in the village.

Kettle Holm, Church Wynd, late 19th century, is emphatically High Victorian with gables, bays, and dormers to match.

David Wilkie, 1785-1841, one of Scotland's greatest painters, was born at Cults manse where some of his early sketches on the walls of the attic were later destroyed by fire. Almost immediately his genre paintings *Pitlessie Fair*, 1804, and *The Village Politicians*, 1806, met with success and it was these skilled presentations of humble life on which his fame mainly rests. Later his style changed and he turned to portraiture and etching. In 1830 he was made Painter in Ordinary to His Majesty and in 1836 was knighted.

171 **White Croft,** c.1840 (*above*)
On west edge of Balmalcolm , crisply geometric house under beetle-browed eaves supported on rustic columns. Reconstructed 1980 by the Jack Fisher Partnership.

PITLESSIE

Early Pitlessie is recorded pictorially, for ever, in Sir David Wilkie's *Pitlessie Fair*, 1804 (National Galleries of Scotland, Edinburgh). Indeed the distant gable can still be identified: No 12 High Street. Otherwise, Pitlessie is like Newton of Falkland, once much dependent on maltings. **Pitlessie House,** Cupar Road, early 19th century, is an example of refined Georgian coarsened by later additions. **Outbuildings** (former maltings) topped by irregular pantiled roofs. Swept loft openings and forestair are attractive. The ruinous **Bonthrone Maltings,** Cupar Road, 1870, are by R Hamilton-Paterson.

172 **Cults Parish Church,** 1793, is a plain building. The round-headed windows on the south were constructed later. Unusually slim, three-stage tower on west gable with forestair. The marble bas-reliefs beside the pulpit should be noted: Sir David Wilkie, 1841, Samuel Joseph, and Revd David Wilkie and wife (the artist's parents), 1833, Francis Chantry. The **Manse,** 1795, has been modified since 1927 fire, but **doocot,** early 16th century, is unusually well preserved.

173 **Crawford Priory**
(originally modest Crawford Lodge, c.1758)
The glory has departed from this gutted shell. The taste remains of a Gothic confection of assorted flavours – Gothic castellated, Gothic

Crawford Priory – the Stable Block

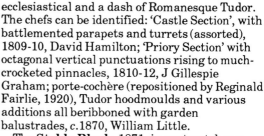

Above *Crawford Priory.* Below *Scotstarvit*

ecclesiastical and a dash of Romanesque Tudor. The chefs can be identified: 'Castle Section', with battlemented parapets and turrets (assorted), 1809-10, David Hamilton; 'Priory Section' with octagonal vertical punctuations rising to much-crocketed pinnacles, 1810-12, J Gillespie Graham; porte-cochère (repositioned by Reginald Fairlie, 1920), Tudor hoodmoulds and various additions all beribboned with garden balustrades, *c.*1870, William Little.

The **Stable Block**, 1871, in contrast, has a unity of style – symmetric Baronial.

174 **Edenwood**, early 19th century, small Georgian mansion. **Home Farm Steading**, early 19th century, has stylish symmetry, with flanking pavilions and low link blocks.

Eden Valley narrows and the plain, south of the river, disappears. The route to the valley of Craigrothie and Ceres Burns climbs the Garlie Bank and enjoys a magnificent view west across the Howe of Fife.

175 **Scotstarvit**, early 17th century
Sited in saddle between Tarvit and Walton Hills, a splendid plain ashlar towerhouse complete with newelstair jamb. Some claim that the lower part of the tower is earlier, *c.*1500. Sir John Scot, who bought the estate from Alexander Inglis in 1611, was thought to be reponsible for work above the double-corbelled parapet executed in 1627, i.e. the crowstepped caphouse and lucarned spire over stair. Kitchen must have been relegated to an outhouse.

176 **Hill of Tarvit** (Colour page C3)
Formerly Wemyss Hall or Upper Tarvit, 1696 It was radically altered in 1905-7 by Sir Robert Lorimer. Sir William Bruce, Master of Works to Charles II, is said to have made the original

design which later acquired Victorian backwings (still identifiable). Round the south and west fronts Lorimer wrapped an uncharacteristic French-style house (though some details were to reappear in his extensions to University Library, St Andrews). The classical south front with bowed projecting wings he complemented with terraced gardens (stepped and balustraded). Each main room had a specific style to suit the magnificent collection of furniture of his client, F B Sharp. **Stable block**, late 18th/early 19th century, has pedimented centre plus pavilions.

Hill of Tarvit: Above left *Garden Gate.* Above *Detail of south front.* Below left *Ceres*

Sir John Scott, Director of Chancery, bought the estate (Scott's) Tarvett from Alexander Inglis in 1611. In 1654 Sir John paid for the sixth volume of Blaeu's maps, containing work of Timothy Pont, the Scottish cartographer, thereby *'at length our Scotland presents itself to the world'* (Gordon of Straloch). He was also the author of the lampoon (published 84 years after his death) *The Staggering State of Scots Statesmen.* His brother-in-law, Drummond of Hawthornden, spent much time at Scotstarvit writing his history of the Jameses.

CERES

Made a Burgh of Barony in 1620. Once described as *'the most attractive village in Scotland'* (George Scott-Moncrieff), it owes much to its Green, the central burnside open space where the Annual Fairs were held.

Parish Church, Main Street, 1805-6, Alexander Leslie
Plain rectangle with arched windows. Tower, crenellated with obelisk corner pinnacles; 1851-2, Hugh Birrell, added a spire on lanky octagonal base. In kirkyard is stone-slated **Lindsay Vault**, 17th century, perhaps

Beside Garlie Bank was the bloodless Battle of Cupar Muir in 1559. The troops of the Queen Regent (Mary of Guise, mother of Mary Queen of Scots) under their French commander, Duc d'Oisel, confronted those of the Lords of the Congregation (the Reformers). The Earl of Crawford managed to persuade the two sides to sign a truce whereby the French troops would withdraw from Fife. It proved a turning point in the history of the establishment of the Protestant religion in Scotland.

'The Provost', Ceres

Wishart

When Ceres was a Burgh of Barony, from 1620, under the Hopes of Craighall the Weigh House served as Burgh tolbooth and Barony Courts were convened there. The 'jougs' (hinged iron collar chained to wall) for the retention of wrongdoers on market day is still at the doorway.

originally attached to an earlier church. **Parish Church Hall/Session House**, 1868, by William Younger, is a skilfully planned, two-storey with Session House at kirkyard level and Hall, originally Hearse House (archway still exists), at street level.

Main Street is a mixture of 18th century and 19th century with 20th-century intrusions, e.g. **Nos 17-19,** plain mid-19th century, and **No 15, Plum Tree Cottage**, 18th century, rebuilt early 19th century with keyblock doorway. **No 54**, mid-19th century, is high proportioned with interesting overdoor panels of masonic insignia and weavers' tools. **Kimberley, No 33**, early 19th century, is the former Schoolmaster's house with schoolroom under same roof but at raised floor level.

The **Provost**, 18th century, re-erected 1939, the village mascot, a toby-jug figure, set in niche said to be a 17th-century fireplace.

Fife Folk Museum, High Street, reconstructed 1969, Cunningham, Jack, Fisher & Purdom Although single-storey street elevation, this two-storey development skilfully incorporates the quaint **Weigh House**, 17th century (complete with overdoor panel depicting scales and inscribed *'God Bless the Just'*) and a pair of 18th-century weavers' houses. Opposite, the **Annexe**, 1984, Hurd Rolland & Partners, is uncompromising monopitch on rubble-stonework.

St John's Masonic Lodge, 1765, is the oft-chosen backdrop to the much-photographed 17th-century Bishop Bridge, low parapeted and cobbled. **Croft House**, North Croft Dyke, late 18th century, assumed its Jacobean dress in 1910. **Baltilly**, *c*.1780, a quintessential, small, plain mansion relaxing in its policies. The main front is framed by cornice and quoins. The Doric doorway has a good fanlight.

Saughtree Cottage, Bridgend. Carved figures on north skew. **Catherine Bank**, Bridgend, early 19th century, Georgian with Ionic doorway, has older ancilleries – crowstepped 18th-century **Coachman's House** and fine 18th-century outhouse, with stone-framed gable doocot (best seen from Back Latch). **Bridgend House**, early 19th century, is a plain version of Catherine Bank.

Left *Fife Folk Museum.* Below left *Panel over door to Weigh House.*

Left *Baltilly.* Below *Fife Folk Museum.* Bottom *St John's Masonic Lodge and Bishop Bridge*

Dura Den

Craighall *(above, before
demolition)*, early 17th century,
modified 1697-9, finally demolished
1955, probably Sir William Bruce.
This enchanting fragment used to
reward those who hiked up
Craighall Den. One entered the site
by Renaissance-style remains of gate
tower, 1657. Only the front wall of
the house survived, like a classical
stage flat in a rural setting. A two-
tiered, three-arched loggia on
channelled lower storey, flanked by
square projections, was surmounted
by a magnificent segmental
pediment with cartouche.

St Andrews Road provides a variety of
symmetrical fronts, e.g. **St Anne's**, early 19th
century, with slim cast-iron columns.
St Helen's, *c.*1840, with original 'lying' panes.
Almac, Windsor and St Margaret's,
Anstruther Road, 19th century, have a pleasing
frontage but end store complete with gable stair,
doocot and finial is the pièce de résistance.

Rockmount, Pitscottie, mid-19th century, is a
picturesque Victorian villa sitting on elevated
terrace. Neatly planned stable block.

177**Blebo House**, early 19th century. Given 'added
stature' by exposure of sunken basement to the
south, 1903, James Findlay – also Baronial
expansion to north.

178**Muir of Blebo**, Blebocraigs, 1988,
Robert Steedman
Stone and pantiled award-winning house. *'Sits
on a hillock as if it had been there for centuries ...
with French or Tuscan overtones'*.
RIBA Jury Report.

DURA DEN (Colour page C3)
This deep wooded gorge held in its yellow
sandstone one of the richest collections of
fossilised fish ever discovered. It remains a place
of abiding interest to geologists. For the best
part of a century, the Dura Burn powered jute-
spinning mills.

Below *Denhall*

179**Dura House**, mid 18th century
This plain, three-storey block, high on the east
bank of the Dura Burn, was engulfed by
pretentious Baronial additions in 1861 by John
Milne. The crowstepped gables bartizaned at
every angle added weight, not style. **Grove
House**, Dura Den, mid 19th century, is Scottish

Jacobean on a mini-Baronial scale. **Denhall,**
late 18th century, is delightfully original with
round-headed windows on all elevations, some so
tall as to serve two storeys. Shapely chimney
gablet and end stacks.

KEMBACK
A small peaceful community high above tree-
shaded traffic-pounded Dura Den. **Old Parish
Church,** *'built 1582, enlarged 1760, preserved
1960'* – only two walls and two gables.
80**Kemback House,** early 18th century, stands
where the Den widens into a parkland of mature
trees. Baronial treatment in 1907 introduced
gablets and angle turrets. **Lodge,** *c.*1830-40:
overhanging eaves, decorative bargeboards, and
'lying' panes make this a fine period example.

Robert Lindsay of Pitscottie,
*c.*1500-65, wrote the *Chronicles of
Scotland, 1436-1565.* Although not
entirely reliable his graphic eye for
detail brings to life incidents in the
reigns from James I to Mary Queen
of Scots.

*Eden Valley – view towards
Hopetoun Monument from above
Cupar*

Eden Valley (north)
Between the River Eden and the North Uplands
of Fife are imposing farms, historic burghs, and
quaint villages. It is an area rich in buildings –
from magnificent castles to primitive weaving
sheds.

GATESIDE
Near the west boundary of the Kingdom, a small
community once aptly named Edenshead.
Edenshead Church, 1823, is a plain rectangle
with minute birdcage-belfry. **Brig House,** late
18th century, still pleasing with swept dormers
and railed steps. Relates well to small bridge,
1784, over Morton Burn. **Gardener's House,**
1752, and two **weaving sheds** stepped up the
slope form a picturesque group.

**In Strathmiglo, Kirklands and
Templelands** districts reflect the
historic division of land between the
church and the Knights Templar.

97

Strathmiglo Town Hall Steeple

STRATHMIGLO
A 16th-century Burgh of Barony. By the early 19th century hand-weaving prospered, and later the power-loom took over. Today the inhabitants can still bleach their clothes on the village green. It is located in a red sandstone region and red stone walls are much in evidence.

Parish Church, 1783-4, George Kilgour
Round-headed windows in a plain block. The pyramid-roofed belfry, unusually, is not corbelled but supported on full-height projection. Its scroll skewputts feature on many old buildings in the village. The red sandstone porch and vestry, c.1925, detract.

Town Hall Steeple, 1734
Parapet is balustraded in typical 16th/17th-century Fife fashion with refinements, e.g. walls are subtly battered and there is a convexity on the octagonal broach spire. Originally, the ground floor contained the town's cells, bypassed by attractive forestair, which still leads direct to the first-floor level and the mid-19th-century Town Hall beyond.

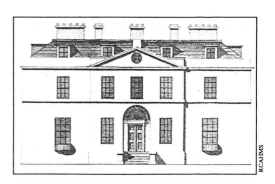

Sir William Scott of Balwearie on whom James V conferred the lands of Cairnie (Wester Strathmiglo) hastily constructed Strathmiglo Castle. He was anxious to have a residence close to Falkland Palace where he could entertain the King. In fact the King nicknamed the building *'Cairnie Flappit'* and by 1734 it was in ruins. The one good outcome of this early example of 'jerry-building' was that it proved a valuable quarry from which to build the handsome Town Hall Steeple, Strathmiglo.

Pitlour, 1783-4, Robert Mylne (*above*)
A splendid mansion confirms A E Richardson's verdict – his style *'combined elegance with restraint'*. The red ashlar and yellow dressings emphasise a classic formality, which, through the arched entrance, is comprehensively developed in the halls, staircase and public rooms. The ancillary buildings show scant respect for the precepts of the mansion: **stable block**, c.1760, quadrangular with Venetian tendencies; **Gardener's House**, small-scale (early 19th-century) Gothick; **West Lodge**,

typical (mid-19th-century) Victorian; **South Lodge**, c.1840, noteworthy Greek Revival.

AUCHTERMUCHTY

This ancient burgh received its Charter in 1517. It was famous for its hand-looms (once numbering over 1000) and its thatched roofs (from the rushes at Lindores Loch). But the last loom stopped weaving in 1912 and thatch has all but disappeared.

32**Parish Church**, Croft, 1779-81, Robert Wilkie Another plain block with round-headed windows redeemed by a graceful six-columned belfry, the capping curves to a pinnacle. Later additions do not enhance. Only **No 20 High Street** (late-18th century with Venetian windows) interrupts a good 19th-century façade at **Nos 12-28**.

33**Town House**, High Street, 1728 Soaring square tower with balustraded parapet enclosing plain, sharp, pyramid spire not only satisfies civic aspirations but is a landmark for the district. Victorian 'improvements' saddled tower with doorway and block with dormers.

Opposite, the **High Street** expands into the old market place – **The Cross**. Where the Mercat Cross once stood is the **War Memorial**, 1919-20, R Fairlie, of classical rigidity.

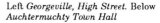

Left *Georgeville, High Street.* Below *Auchtermuchty Town Hall*

34**Georgeville**, 13 High Street, early 18th century, closes the east end of The Cross –

Auchtermuchty in 1837, drawn by T. Allom

'The Modern Movement lands in Fife!' – Conversion of former railway station for an engineering firm

classical frontage given Tudor embellishments 185in the 19th century. The **Boar's Head**, early 19th century, a former coaching inn, and **Nos 17,19, 21 High Street** share a moulded eaves-course and form an impressive north façade to 186The Cross. **Macduff House**, High Street, 1597, is an outstanding building, converted to an L-plan by 17th-century south wing. Fortunately, 18th- and 19th-century alterations and additions have failed to spoil its original character. Inside are interesting 18th-century panelling, and 18716th/17th-century staircases. **Parliament Square**, another pleasing expansion of the High Street, is lined with an assortment of 18th-188century houses (mostly modernised). **Braehead House**, 51 High Street, 1772, is worthy of note; 17th-century gateway rebuilt 1963.

Dark whinstone walls with freestone dressings 189are a feature of many houses, e.g. **Nos 36, 38, 40 Simpson Terrace**, late 18th/early 19th century, where two houses have artisan classical porches. Auchtermuchty's architecture provides many 190contrasts, e.g. the much-dormer-headed **Madras House**, Madras Road, mid-19th century; traditional irregular fenestration on Crosshills 191frontage of **Dovecot House**, 18th century. 192**Royal Hotel**, Cupar Road, mid-19th century, an original double pile, marks the centre of another interesting group. On the **Low Road, Hollies Hotel**, late 18th century; **Southport House**,

93*c.*1800, then **Nos 6-18 Eden Place** and **The Anchorage**, all early 19th century. Throughout, the quirked stop chamfer at openings is a 94distinctive feature. **Cameron House**, 26 Cupar Road, 18th century; note sculptured head at skewputt and 19th-century doorway.

95**Myres Castle** (once a tower house), *c.*1540 Originally it comprised two rectangular parallel blocks (joined at one angle to form Z-plan). Round towers are at diagonally opposite corners. Additions and alterations have diminished the impact of the north block but the south block has literally grown in stature. In 1616 an extra storey was added and two extra storeys to its round tower, thereby creating a dramatic ashlar terminal, which, today, is the hallmark of a castle, the rest of which is harled.

96Symmetric Georgian **Rossie** farmhouse, 19th century, has been overwhelmed by additions. Its 18th-century steading has, however, retained 97open arcades and cast-iron columns. **Lumquat,** *c.*1880, is refreshingly Jacobean and **Cornhill,** *c.*1860, Peddie & Kinnear, still keeps its compact Baronial design.

98**Rossie House**, pre-1700 The original house was extended *c.*1700 (three-storey plain west section), and then replaced, *c.*1767, by a splendid three-window bow east section. Harling with exposed corner pilasters and margins gives it a unity.

99**Kinloch House**, dates from *c.*1700; in 1859 Charles Kinnear applied an exuberant Scots Baronial casing. A massive steep-gabled tower marks the entrance and it is flanked by crowsteps, conical bartizans and sinuous Dutch roofs. Sir Robert Lorimer's extensions, 1921-3, included ogee-roofed oriel.

COLLESSIE

This hamlet clusters round a knoll dominated by the church. There are still relics of its weaving past. The **Parish Church**, 1838-9, R & R Dickson, is too big for the hamlet but just right for the rural parish. Prominently pinnacled tower commands wide views across the Howe. Under a weeping willow the **Kirkyard Dyke**, 1609, contains a Late Gothic gateway. **Strad Cottage**, 1839, has stone canopies over the windows. On the ground, west of the Church, are two late 18th-century detached **weaving sheds,**

Myres Castle (*above*) originally was surrounded by a marsh. In early 16th century its owner, John Scrymgeour, Master of the King's Works, was employed in the construction of the Palaces of Falkland and Holyroodhouse. It is said that Mary, Queen of Scots often rested here after exhausting wild boar hunts in the Howe. Later the castle became a refuge for Covenanters.

Reginald Fairlie (1883-1952), architect, was born in Myres Castle. He began his professional career under Sir Robert Lorimer before going to London then travelled in France and Italy. He set up his own practice in Edinburgh in 1909. One of his first commissions was St James' RC Church, St Andrews, 1909-10. In all, he was responsible for over 30 new churches designed in his own special Scots Baronial/Romanesque style. In his many restorations he was always sympathetic to the original design and reluctant to impose his own style – a marked contrast to Sir Robert Lorimer.

Top *Rose Cottage, Collessie.* Centre
Collessie School Gate. Above *West
Lodge and gate piers, Ramornie,
Ladybank*

one dated 1662. **Rose Cottage** is a splendid L-plan thatched house carefully formed out of three late 18th-century weavers' cottages. The **Primary School**, 1846, R & R Dickson, is a Gothic composition integrating school and house and featuring a belfry. The pergola is modern – so is the sign 'Schoolhouse' but its style is appropriate!

LADYBANK

This burgh (Charter 1878) is a newcomer. Only after the Howe of Fife was adequately drained did its linen trade develop (early 19th century). Like Thornton, it was not really established until it became a railway junction. First it was on the main Burntisland/Tayport line and then by the mid-19th century there were branch lines to Newburgh and Milnathort.

Parish Church, Church Street, 1874-6, Peddie & Kinnear
Well-buttressed geometric Gothic – its broach spire containing large lucarnes. **Ladybank Pumping Station**, Beeches Road, 1908, (Colour page C3) is a rarity in contrasting brickwork, enthusiastically detailed with great round-headed arches, pilasters and corbels. **Ladybank Railway Station**, Commercial Crescent, is probably the oldest Scottish station which remains virtually unaltered. **West Block**, 1847-8, Grainger & Miller, with the same Italianate style adopted by Grainger, the previous year at Markinch, includes integral Station Master's house. Cast-iron columns with acanthus capitals support low-pitched platform canopy. **East Block**, late 19th century, built of modest brick and timber redeemed by enriched fretted valance at canopy. Detached **Lodge/Ticket Office**, *c.*1847, has Baronial aspirations. Nearby, the **Railway Engine Shed**, and **Workshop**, *c.*1850, have diamond-paned windows and the shed has distinctive round-arched openings.

West Lodge, Ramornie House (now demolished), mid-19th century, is a diminutive Baronial composition, but the **Gate Piers**, *c.*1780, have spectacularly tall pyramidal caps.

200 **Melville House**, 1697-1703, James Smith
Pennant in 1776 refers to *'Melvil ... a fine house, the nine window front'*. It was Fife's first mansion styled symmetrically in classical detail on a grandiose scale. Its resemblance to Kinross House suggests Sir William Bruce's influence,

doubtless pruned by Smith to suit the tight purse-strings of his client, the 1st Earl of Melville. From afar distinctive features are its height, emphasised by massive central lantern and towering chimney stacks, and the precise symmetry of its bleak sparsely embellished elevations. The nine-bay north and south fronts match as do the six-bay east and west fronts. Twin blocks, screen walls and gazebos form the south forecourt. Once a beech-lined avenue, 1km long on the main axis of the mansion led to the original gate (now abandoned) and was then considered one of the finest approaches in Scotland. Extensive low offices and court to the east have been discreetly adapted and extended to provide educational facilities for boys who now use the mansion as residential accommodation.

Top *Melville House.* Above *Melville House doocot*

Doocot, west of Melville Gates roundabout, *c.*1770, converted windmill, tapering cylinder rises to curved, crowstepped flanks.

201**Monimail Tower**, 1578 (*overleaf*)
This unexpected and interesting fragment of a residence used by Bishops of St Andrews since the 14th century is incorporated into the original walled garden of Melville House. Believed to be the north-west tower of a quadrangular palace it stands four storeys high with parapet incorporating Renaissance roundels (as at Falkland Palace) and caphouse. There is still 18th-century pine panelling in upper chamber.

James Smith, *c.*1645-1731, originally studied for the priesthood but resigned and travelled on behalf of Sir William Bruce. In 1679 he married daughter of Robert Mylne, Master Mason to the Crown of Scotland and succeeded Sir William Bruce as Surveyor of the King's Works in Scotland in 1683. His major buildings in Fife are Raith House, 1692-4, and Melville House, 1697-1703. Although his completed works confirm that Smith was a student of Sir William Bruce some of his drawings suggest that he was a pioneer of British Palladianism.

In adjacent **Monimail Kirkyard** are fragments of the pre-Reformation Church (abandoned 1797).

202**Monimail Parish Church** (*above*), 1794-7, Thomas Falconer
A simple T-plan with elegant touches – Venetian window, ogee tracery, ball urns on skewputts. Slender four-stage Gothic tower, 1811, by Robert Hutchison (J Gillespie Graham was adviser). The Melville gallery, semi-octagonal plan, is supported on Tuscan columns.

The last tenant of Monimail Palace (*above*) was **Archbishop Hamilton,** who, it was claimed, was cured of asthma by the Italian astrologer Cardan who advised drinking from nearby (Cardan's) well. Hamilton failed to persuade Mary, Queen of Scots not to trust herself to Elizabeth Tudor and he himself was hanged in Stirling Castle in 1571.

LETHAM
A hillside village with simple road system in the form of a cross. The approach from the A914 is lined with late 18th/early 19th-century cottages, many altered and modernised out of recognition. The west branch, **West End**, comprises 19th-century houses. The east branch includes **Letham Lands Farm House**, late 18th century, now radically altered and obscured by pebbledash. Behind is the farm **doocot**, 17th/18th century, a dainty cylinder corbelled to square above ratcourse. Up **School Brae** are two more 17th/18th-century lectern doocots.

Fernie Castle

203**Fernie Castle**, from 16th-century
A tower house to which every succeeding century

has made identifiable contributions. First, the plain tower acquired a stair jamb and a circular tower corbelled to square (angled to the jamb). By the early 18th century an east wing had materialised and, c.1815, a west wing (later raised to two storeys). When it became a hotel in the 20th century the extensions continued and the stylistic complexity exacerbated. Across the meadow, the two spacious classical courts of the **stables** and the **kennels** are early 19th century.

4**Cunnoquhie**, originally 18th century; remodelled 1892, probably by Watherson & Sons An elegantly classical mansion with a semicircular Ionic-columned entrance portico on the east front. The unusual five-bay west wing features a Tuscan colonnade which supports a first-floor arcaded balustrade. Internally the elliptical-shaped hall and cupola over staircase are worthy of note. **Stable Block**, early 19th century, features a cylindrical clock-tower with finialed dome. The **Lodge**, early 19th century, manages to look both classical and picturesque.

Cunnoquhie – stable block

Over Rankeillor

05**Over Rankeillor**, 1796-1800, James MacLaren Supervised by Andrew Laing, it is a handsome, copybook, classical mansion. Central doorway, c.1883, relocated on four-bay east front. The nine-bay **stable block**, c.1800, reflects the south front of the mansion. **Home Farm**, 1819-20, continues classical symmetry with emphasis on centre and end bays; now the Scottish Deer Centre.

06**Stratheden Hospital** (originally Lunatic Asylum), opened 1866 – a complex of spectacular growth. Original stoneblock 1863-5 by Peddie & Kinnear ingeniously achieves symmetry on sloping site.

Hopetoun Monument, Lindifferan Hill, 1826 – a landmark for the entire valley of the Eden, in the form of a giant (almost 28m high) Doric column. It was erected in memory of Sir John Hope of Over Rankeillor who successfully assumed command in the Peninsular War after the death of Sir John Moore at Corunna in 1809.

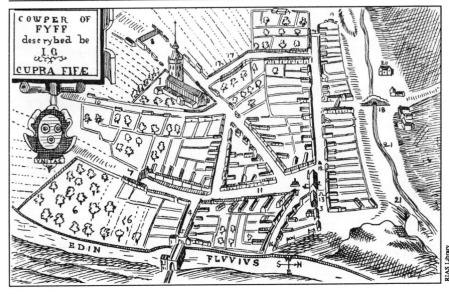

Top *Mid 17th-century Cupar.* Centre right *The Cross and St Catherine Street – Cupar's civic frontage*

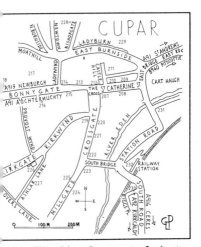

The oldest document referring to **Cupar** appears to be a Grant by Robert II, 1381 (later confirmed by James I in 1428), which permitted the people of Cupar, who traded with Flanders, a free port at Guardbridge at the mouth of the River Eden. Cupar's wealth at this time is revealed by its generous contributions to David II's ransom in 1357, Royal Expenses, 1435, and Queen Mary's dowry, 1449.

CUPAR

Old maps record crossings of the River Eden and Lady Burn from which radiated roads to all parts of the Kingdom of Fife. From here the Earls (from 1213), then the Sheriffs and eventually the County Council of Fife chose to rule. Cupar remains a busy market town but the administrative centre now has only District (North-East Fife) status. At the historic hub of this Royal Burgh (Charter 1328), the intersection of Crossgate and Bonnygate, stands the **Market Cross**, its original circular shaft, 1683, surmounted by a unicorn. To the east, a Haussmann-like Provost carved St Catherine Street at the expense of the Old Tolbooth (coat of arms now incorporated in Castlehill Centre) and a Dominican Monastery. Master plan, 1810, of the new street was by J Gillespie Graham but most of the building work was directed by Robert Hutchison.

07**Town House,** St Catherine Street, 1815-17, Robert Hutchison
A three-storey bow corner, crowned with dome and clock cupola. A robust Doric doorway marks its street entrance.

08**County Buildings,** St Catherine Street, *c.*1812-17, Robert Hutchison
The original central section is an excellent example of Local Authority classical. A balcony (for official proclamations) sits above a Doric entrance. On the flanking façades two-storey Doric pilasters stand on a rusticated ground-floor storey. To the east, another five bays (*c.*1817), still classical but less elaborate, were subsequently gutted in 1836 by William Burn. An elegant **Sheriff Courtroom** was formed with vaulted ceiling.

09**St James Church,** St Catherine Street, 1866, Rowand Anderson
Early neo-Gothic. Internal screen, rood and reredos by Sir Robert Lorimer. **Nos 10, 12** and 10**14 St Catherine Street,** *c.*1816-25, Robert Hutchison, is a fine façade; **10** and **12** constituting a 'reflected' composition while **14** has Ionic column porch on Castlehill frontage.

11**Castlehill Centre,** Castlehill
Site of Cupar Castle, buildings have educational origins. **East Block** (originally Cupar Academy), 1806, in institutional classical style with central pediment (over door, coat of arms from Old Tolbooth); **South Block** (an extension to what was, by then, Madras Academy), 1844-6, is a large-scale version of East Block with giant orders. Basement storey on south elevation incorporates arched windows of late 18th-century Guildhall; **North Block**, 1867, is a typical small school of Victorian era.

12**Corn Exchange, Tower,** 1861-2, Campbell Douglas & Stevenson
A distinctive silhouette on the Cupar skyline where the upper section of the tall lucarned roof sits on fretwork inset.

The beginning of **Bonnygate** offers a variety of

On the **Castle Hill** (*above*) was a field where morality plays were performed. On Whitsun 1535 it saw the premiere of *Ane Pleasant Satyre of the Thrie Estaitis* by Sir David Lindsay of the Mount (estate on the hill surmounted by the Hopetoun Monument). This satire (the earliest extant example of Scottish drama) full of humour, good sense and worldly wisdom, with some of its sharpest shafts directed at the clergy, is said to have been more effective and done more for the Reformation than all the sermons of John Knox. Sir Walter Scott wrote of it:

'The flash of that satiric rage
Which, bursting on the early stage
Branded the vices of the age
And broke the keys of Rome.'

Corn Exchange Tower

29-31 Bonnygate

19th-century treatments. At **Nos 3-5**, *c*.1840, bowed dormers add interest; on **23-25** (former Stratheden Temperance Hotel, *c*.1800) the embellishment is restrained while **29-31** has elegant arched shop windows with cast-iron balconies above; **43** (on corner of Lady Wynd), 1871, is a dramatic statement by James MacLaren of arched ground-floor windows, corbelled upper floor and gablet dormers. On south side of Bonnygate the fenestration is regular with quoins and cornices at **6, 16, 18, 20** and pedimented window at **26**; **30-32**, 1912, attracts attention with red stone dressings and rounded angle which develops into crenellated tower.

Freemasons Hall, 72-4 Bonnygate, 1811, aspires to the grandiose with end bays pilastered in two-storey coupled Doric. **St John's Church,** Bonnygate, 1875-8, Campbell Douglas & Sellars, demonstrates the verticality of Early Pointed Style, needle-like lucarned spire and angle pinnacles.

Preston Lodge with the spire of St John's Church beyond

Preston Lodge, 95 Bonnygate, 1623
In 1660, *'The Laird of Airdrie depairted out of this life at his house in Cupar'*, which he had built, and which latterly continued to moulder (until 1989, when remedial work started). On

Moathill Road its north boundary wall is graced with late-17th-century gate piers adorned with fluted pilasters. The projecting outer bays (original) of the south front have pilastered and moulded windows. Their string-courses, once continuous across the frontage, have been interrupted by later façade, c.1770, built between projections. Much of the interior detailing dates from 1690s.

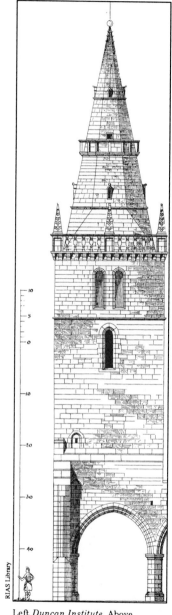

Features on the south side of Bonnygate include **No 82**, rebuilt early 19th century, with eccentric fenestration; **94**, an original shop front and fanciful windowheads; at the corner of Provost Wynd is the solid, rusticated **98**.

Crossgate runs south from the Market Cross. Outstanding amid the humdrum façades of the ¹⁹west side is the individualistic **Duncan Institute**, 33-35 Crossgate, 1870-1, John Milne, commissioned by Mrs Duncan, Edengrove, as a Mechanics' Institute *'for the working classes of Cupar'*. Styled enthusiastically in a mixture of Gothic, Scottish and Flemish its main feature is the twisted spire supported (visually) by snub-²⁰nosed bartizans. **No 32-34 Crossgate**, mid 19th century, still retains some Renaissance grandeur and evidence of fine (though much worn) ²²¹carving; **No 46**, Trustee Savings Bank, 1901, William Burrell, has pompous Renaissance ²²details; **No 80, Chancellor's House**, late 17th century (remodelled mid 18th century), was saved from destruction by conversion into flats in the late 20th century. Once a first-rate town

Left *Duncan Institute.* Above *Measured drawing of St Michael's tower by J Russell Walker*

109

Old Parish (St Michael of Tarvit) Church, Kirkgate, Cupar

Wishart

house (used as a manse 1773-1824), still well detailed with splayed margins and projecting dressings. Beyond the commercial area of 223 Crossgate lies **Barony**. **No 1**, early 19th century, has quoins, cornice and delightful fanlight; **No 3**, also early 19th century, small 224 scale and plain. **Eden Villa**, *c*.1840, enjoys amenity of a walled front garden. Opposite, 225 **Millgate Terrace**, mostly early 19th century, is neat and **No 1** is graced with Venetian doorway.

226 **Old Parish (St Michael of Tarvit) Church**, Kirkgate, Hay Bell (architect & builder) An impressive mongrel resulting from the linking of a 1415 tower (survivor of the 'new parish church' founded by the Priory of St Andrews) and a 1785 church. In 1620, the original rugged tower was increased in height and within a finialed balustrade a handsome broached spire was provided with tiers of lucarnes and unusual intermediate gallery (all at the expense of the minister, Revd William Scott). Remnants of the earlier church adjacent to the tower were incorporated in new Session House. The church itself is plain save for small Venetian windows and urn finials at gables. In segmental arched niche in west wall is 15th-century tomb with recumbent figure of 'Muckle Fernie'. North porch added 1811.

227 **Provost Scott Court**, Ashlar Lane, late 20th century Sheltered Housing development makes good use of existing stone buildings. **Bell-Baxter Annexe** (former Kirkgate School), Lovers Lane, *c*.1860, is an elaborate variation on Venetian window by James MacLaren & Son, 1881. **St Columba**, Kirkgate, 1964, Peter Whiston; drum-on-cone roof with bare expressed frame, marred by inept entrance. **Nos 34-40 Kirkgate**, late 18th/early 19th century, a traditional group; note grotesque head.

Cupar, compared with other Fife towns, is particularly well endowed with detached, early 19th-century Georgian-style houses. There is **Westfield House**, Westfield Road, *c*.1810, with its unusually high parapet (bowed wings, *c*.1825); **Roseville**, Bank Street, early 19th 228 century, slim window margins; **Bishopgate House**, Bishopgate, *c*.1810, a contrast in red 229 ashlar and yellow dressings; **Marybank**, East Burnside, *c*.1830, with its own bridge over Lady Burn, and flyover steps leading to entrance with fanlight; **Eden Park** (flatted 1984), McInnes Place, early 19th century, once enjoyed its own parkland; single-storey wings formed part of original composition. **Southfield**, Ceres Road, *c.*1835, spectacularly sandwiched between pedimented elevations. Garden front features coupled pilasters and couchant lions.

Knox Cottages, South Road, 1835-6 Small-scale, symmetrical composition built as almshouses by Robert Hutchison to design provided by London architect.

0**Rosemount**, Riggs Place, *c.*1810 Highly individual Gothic villa; narrow two-storey centre with elaborate fanlight over doorway, flanked by bow-fronted single-storey wings with semiconical roofs.

Above *Rosemount, Riggs Place.* Below *Watts*

1**Watts**, 1813-14, J Gillespie Graham Incredibly a former prison designed for site at east end of St Catherine Street where War Memorial is now located. Exceptional classical composition with two-storey Doric columns.

2**Railway Station**, 1847, Thomas Grainger Distinguished, fully worked out, symmetrical design in broad-eaved Italianate style. Two-storey centre with graceful oriel window has matching wings, flanking pavilions and single-storey links.

The 1930s style made little impact on conservative Cupar. One example is **Firbank**, Brighton Road, 1936, by William Guild. Originally a flat roof facilitated flexible planning with rounded external walls but technical inadequacies have now decreed a pitched roof.

Substantial estates and farms circle Cupar. Some mansions have been demolished but surviving buildings testify to past magnificence. 233To the south, **Tarvit**, *c.*1790 (demolished 1963); **steading**, an impressive 11 bays dominated by octagonal clocktower with spire which many a church would be proud of; to the north, **Kilmaron Castle**, *c.*1820, J Gillespie Graham (demolished mid-20th century); **stable block**, *c.*1820, J Gillespie Graham – a life-size toy-town fort in castellated Gothic. At the burgh boundary stands **Dalgairn**, *c.*1770. Broad curving steps lead to Doric-columned entrance.

234 On the ridge, to the north, are **Hilton**, *c.*1795, refined with 19th-century pedimented wings (bowed gables feature at early 19th-century 235**Lodge**) and **Cairnie Lodge**, *c.*1770, a plain laird's house with early 19th-century bow-fronted wings and suffering from 20th-century additions. Its 19th-century **Home Farm** retains its ogival-roofed tower as central focal point. **Lodge**, early 19th century, is a study in classical detail to the tip of its anthemion finial.

DAIRSIE
(formerly Osnaburgh and Dairsie Muir)
Development of turnpike road and good supply of well water encouraged the growth of Dairsie, a village of 18th- and 19th-century weavers. Some cottages still have characteristic additional windows of the weavers' dwelling.

St Mary's Old Parish Church

236**St Mary's Old Parish Church**, 1621
Hosts a hodgepodge of Gothic and classical, the undoubted success of which defies analysis. The

conversion of the original lead flat roof (the grotesque mask drain spouts for which still exist) to a piended roof (1794) reconciled the church to the overbearing corner belfry. Octagonal form continues through balustrade and faceted spire. Plain stepped buttresses define the bays of windows plate-traceried to ape the Gothic style. Although it fails to recapture, as intended, the beauty of a Gothic pre-Reformation church its modest charm delights. The fragmentary **Dairsie Castle** was a late 16th-century Z-plan palace: surviving sections of corner towers with oval gun loops.

Dairsie Bridge, *c.*1530, spans the Eden in three graceful round arches with ribbed soffits and massive cut-waters; later modification to parapet to form refuge.

Dairsie Kirk, Castle and Bridge by Francis Grose c.1780

Dairsie Village School

Village School, Main Street, County Architect At the west entry to the village stands this commendably modern, flat-roofed, Philip Johnson-inspired design with much glass in slender frames and occasional stone infills one of which contains dates of old and new schools, 1868/1970. Opposite, **Dairsie Memorial Hall**, Main Street, 1922, steep pitched and pantiled Arts & Crafts style.

In Charter dated 1452 James II gave to Bishop of St Andrews the lands of *Craigfudy, Mydilfudy, Wester (Craig)fudy* which occupy the wooded hillside overlooking Dairsie.

Over its early years, **Dairsie Old Church** had a 'mixed press': *'one of the beautifulest little pieces of church work'* and *'the work of a cabinetmaker rather than an architect'*. It is said that David II spent much of his boyhood at **Dairsie Castle** where, in 1335, the Scottish Estates met. Archbishop John Spottiswoode rebuilt it in the grand style and is said to have written his *History of the Church and State of Scotland* within its walls.

237**Craigfoodie**, 18th century, is a well-proportioned block on raised basement. Early 19th-century west front sports Doric-columned entrance and two bowed bays.

238**Middle Foodie**, late 18th/early 19th century, is a plain house with low piended wings. Row of pantiled cottages and wing with arched openings complete delightful group. East of Dairsie

239amidst its acres of fruit is **Pittormie**, 1764, a simple four-bay Georgian farmhouse which received extravagant Victorian Baronial treatment in 1867, John Milne. However, as seems customary, much of the classical symmetry of the **Steading**, 1855, survives intact. Note triangular doocot over pend.

Arts in Fife

240**Pitcullo**, late 16th century (*above*)
Saved from ruin in 1971 by R C Spence, it commands the Eden Estuary from its hillside vantage. An L-plan of traditional form with plain harled walls, corners chamfered and rounded; service stair, a mere ripple on the north elevation. Above the wall head, a profusion of jettied and corbelled detail applied from early 17th century up to the 1980s (by Ian Begg).

LEUCHARS

In an area pervaded with marshes were two knolls: Castle Knowe to the north, where once stood Leuchars Castle (demolished mid-18th century) and Temple Hill, where stands the Parish Church. When, c.1790, the Great Drain was constructed (Sir David Carnegie), the marshes dried up and the village, known appropriately as 'Lochyeords' developed. The rail junction, c.1848, and the establishment of the

RN (1917) and, later, RAF (1920) Station
ensured its continuing prosperity.

Wisbart

McKean/Billings

Parish Church, St Athernase,
Schoolhill, 1183-7
*'The second finest piece of Norman work in the
whole of Great Britain'* is one justifiable verdict
on the apse and chancel. On plan the apse is
stilted (i.e. more than a semicircle) as clearly
illustrated by the configuration of the internal
ribs of the vaulting. By *c*.1700 this vaulting
supported the stone bell turret which replaced
the original timber roof. The octagonal form of
the turret continues up through three stages
and converges on the apex of the pepperpot
stone capping. Time has assuaged this intrusion
and it now is a feature of the church. Worthy of
close study is the two-tiered blind arcading on
chancel (relatively plain) and apse (heavily
embellished); also the magnificent carving at
wallhead corbels and string-courses. Chancel
and sanctuary arches were restored in 1914 by
Reginald Fairlie, who also reinstated the
arcading (damaged by the insertion of a window
in the 17th century). Nave, 1857-8, John Milne,
is Victorian Romanesque as is gable-arch porch.

RIAS Library/Miller

*St Athernase. The tombstone in the
Chancel is to the memory of Dame
Agnes Lyndesay, Lady to William
Bruce of Earshall, 'who in her life
was charitable to the poor and
profitable to that house. Died 1635 of
her age 68, and waiteth here in hope'*

McKean/Billings

Wishart

Earlshall, as drawn by R. W. Billings c.1847. Above The Gate House (See colour page C4)

241 **Earlshall**, 1546, Sir William Bruce and *'completed by his great-grandson William Bruce in 1617'*

Its majesty and romance, miraculously restored in 1891-8 by Sir Robert Lorimer, enchant all who visit it. The core is a 16th-century L-plan tower house with 17th-century dormerheads. A fine entrance and turnpike stair form a re-entrant tower corbelled out to a 17th-century caphouse. At north-east angle is a massive oval-shaped tower complete with turret stair. On the first floor, the Hall has been restored complete with slabbed floor supported on barrel-vaulted lower storey. The Dining Room is defined by Lorimer-designed oak screen based on Falkland Palace model. The painted, boarded ceiling (a semi-elliptical vault) of the second-floor Long Gallery was painstakingly restored by Lorimer.

A high west-facing barmkin wall (which contains the gateway to the entrance courtyard) links the tower house to a small 16th-century tower from which a 17th-century range extends. This range (the former coachman's house and stables) displays typical Lorimer features, excellent masonwork, neatly formed dormers and convenient forestair. The range completes the third side of the entrance courtyard which is open-balustraded to the garden. There, Lorimer created the topiary of yew chessmen. In the north-west corner, the two-storey garden house, c.1900, with distinctive ogee-roof, forestair, and animal carvings.

At the end of the driveway Lorimer's dramatic **Gate House**, c.1900, complete with arched pend and bell-roofed turret, sets the pattern for the delights which lie beyond.

Royal Air Force Station,
from 1911 (when under Army control)
Motley collection of buildings ranging from the small domestic, through barracks institutional up to mammoth hangars of varying vintages.

Old Guard Bridge

GUARDBRIDGE
Another village generated by river crossings – here, over the River Eden and Motray Water. Paper mill (now operating under the name of GB Papers) converted from distillery, 1872, dominates the village. **Willowbank**, c.1830, is a picturesque villa, with V-plan dormers in broad-eaved piended roof matching V-plan bays below.

Old Guard Bridge, early 15th century
A handsome Scottish medieval bridge of six semicircular arches. 'Lie gare brig' was built by Bishop Wardlaw of St Andrews (1404-40), but Archbishop James Beaton (1522-39), whose arms and initials are part of the structure, may have been responsible for some of the repairwork. Great triangular cut-waters have been carried up to form refuges.

ST ANDREWS (Colour page C4)
Legend claims that over 16 centuries ago St Regulus, bearing some of the bones of St Andrew, landed at the rocky promontory known as *Cenn-rigmonnaid*, Head of the King's Mount. Records confirm that four centuries later, in the mid-8th century, a shrine for the miracle-working bones had been founded and St Andrews had become a place of pilgrimage. In due course, the faith of these pilgrims kindled a religious zeal which built a cathedral. For the greater part of 700 years, St Andrews was the ecclesiastical capital of Scotland. The same faith generated a secular power which, symbolised by the **Castle**, the Archbishop's Palace, drew to St Andrews most of the leading characters in Scottish history. The same faith nourished a love of learning which led to the founding of Scotland's oldest university.

Leuchars' association with the 'airborne' began modestly with barrage balloons in the charge of Royal Engineers in 1911. During World War I, in 1917, a basic airfield was established under the aegis of the Royal Navy – a Fleet Training School. In 1920 this was handed over to the Royal Air Force. In 1938 it became part of Coastal Command and after World War II first Fighter Command, 1950, then Strike Command, 1968, took over.

'St Andrews by the Northern Sea
A haunted town it is to me'.
This much-quoted couplet from *Alma Mater* by the multi-talented **Andrew Lang** (1844-1912) distils the gentle nostalgia which for many, still pervades St Andrews. But other poets strike other chords – **George Bruce** (b.1909) wrote in 'A Gateway to the Sea':
'Pause stranger at the porch; nothing beyond
This framing arch of stone, but scattered rocks
And sea and these on the low beach
Original to the cataclysm and the dark.'
and **Tom Scott** (b.1920) 'Brand the Builder':
'Stoupan throu the anvil pend
Gaes Brand
And owre the coort wi the twa-three partan creels,
The birss air fu
O the smell o the sea, and fish, and meltit glue.'

St Andrews has meticulously recorded where its Reformation martyrs were burned. **Paul Craw**, 1433, at paved cross where the Mercat Cross stood at intersection of College and Market Streets.
Patrick Hamilton, 1528, where his initials are set in the cobbles at the pend under St Salvator's Tower.
George Wishart, 1546, where his initials are set in the roadway outside St Andrews Castle.
Martyrs' Monument, The Scores, 1846, commemorates all three and in addition **Henry Forrest**, 1533, and **Walter Myln**, 1558, who were burned outside the cathedral.

Opposite *St Andrews Cathedral: 'Those rent skeletons of pierced wall through which our sea winds moan and murmer . . .' John Ruskin*

The earliest surviving document about **golf** on the St Andrews links was issued in 1552, wherein Archbishop Hamilton reserved to the burgh the rights to *'playing at golf'* on the links adjacent to the *'water of Eden'*. By 1598 Kirk Session Registers record the *'prophaning of the Sabboth day in playing at the gouf efter nune'*. The following year a list of fines was drawn up for those who *'beis fund playand or passis to play at the goufe'* when they should be at Session meetings. In 1754 the Society of St Andrews Golfers (*'twenty two admirers of the ancient and healthful exercise of golf'*) was founded and under the patronage of William IV it became the world-renowned **Royal & Ancient Golf Club** in 1834, the governing authority for the game of golf throughout most of the world. St Andrews premier course, The Old Course (which is not owned by the Royal & Ancient) *'is a perfect example of an original layout of nature, interpreted and completed by beast and man'*. (Sir Guy Campbell)

Within its generous (some say fossilised) medieval plan the town of St Andrews provided the infrastructure for these institutions of religion, government and learning. By the early 16th century it was at the height of its glory. Trade links with the Continent prospered and its great annual Sensie Market drew *two or three hundred vessels*. After the Reformation all three were to go into decline from which only the University (with a struggle) was to recover. Meanwhile the Links had spawned a pastime which would later establish the Royal Burgh (Charter 1620) as the golf centre of the world.

Today St Andrews is still pre-eminently a seat of learning and the Home of Golf. In its own quiet way it satisfies the yearnings of those who seek leisure, full or part-time.

242**Church of the Blessed Mary on the Rock**
A cruciform trace of foundations on a clifftop above the harbour. Nave is 10th/11th century, transepts and choir 13th century. Probably also the site of a 9th-century Culdee house, the earliest place of worship in St Andrews.

243**St Regulus (St Rule's) Church,** 11th century Plain, enigmatic, said to have been built to house the relics of St Andrew. Surviving tower and choir stand within 35m of the cathedral which succeeded it. The 33m *'four-neukit tower'* is a stark tribute to the skill of medieval masons and still contains the lofty arched openings which linked the nave and chancel additions, early 12th century by Bishop Robert. Once it had a spire but not a parapet. Since the 17th century it has had a parapet but no spire.

244**Cathedral Church** (*right*) from 1160
Founded by Arnold, Bishop of St Andrews, and consecrated in 1318 by Bishop Lamberton. With a 14-bay nave, five-bay choir, and transepts and cross tower to match it was planned on a scale unknown, before or since, in Scotland and rivalled the largest churches south of the border. The *'great church'* was in use for about three centuries during which time it suffered severe damage by gale and fire and each time was reconstructed in the contemporary style. By 1560, the Reformation heralded the final downfall, neglect followed and it became a quarry for the local builders.

Despite Dr Johnson's forebodings, 1773, *a Church profaned and hastening to the ground*, the ruins have an enduring quality. For, over the

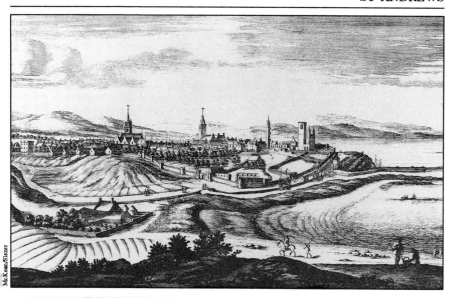

St Andrews has secured a unique niche in history and its citizens jealously guard its architectural heritage. According to R G Cant: *Its series of great medieval buildings and its characteristic domestic architecture of the 16th, 17th and early 18th century ... are in fact without serious rival in Scotland unless it be the Old Town of Edinburgh.* It is also *remarkably well endowed with fine buildings of the next architectural period,* i.e. Georgian/early Victorian. In 1318 Robert the Bruce attended the dedication of St Andrews Cathedral and, with a grant of 100 merks annually, expressed his gratitude *'for the mighty victory vouchsafed to the Scots at Bannockburn by St Andrew, the Guardian of the realm.'* The rectangular, two-storey tower on the sea stretch of the Priory Wall is called the **Haunted Tower**. When the upper apartment was opened in 1868 it was found to be packed with coffins and skeletons, one of which wore white leather gloves, the hallmark of the Ghost of the White Lady. It is reported that she made regular appearances in this area. Her story and those of her fellow apparitions were enthusiastically collected by a St Andrews **Dean of Guild W T Linskill**, 1856-1929.

last three centuries, their shapes have scarcely changed and have become indelibly implanted in the minds of succeeding generations.

Today, a dispassionate survey records only one and a half gables and two walls but these fragments speak volumes giving rise to endless speculation about the stylistic changes during its lengthy construction and its accident-prone lifetime. In the nave wall there is the abrupt change from the round-headed Romanesque to the pointed Gothic window. There is the contrast between the austere Romanesque east gable with the large elevated window inserted by Prior Haldenstone, c.1430, and the west gable, reconstructed in the 14th century, with gableted pinnacles, traceried windows, blind arcading and multi-ordered west doorway – like Dunfermline Abbey.

Priory, c.1236
Little remains except a delineated lawn, although there has been some restoration in red sandstone under the direction of the Marquis of Bute (early 20th century). Excellent 1990 conversion of Frater Undercroft and Warming House, to Visitors' Centre. *Guide book available.*

Precinct Wall, c.14th century
Reconstructed early 16th century, a formidable

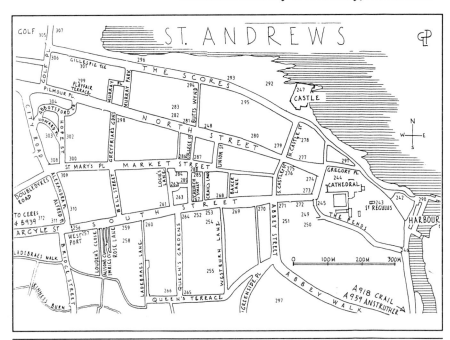

wall, over one kilometre long contained 13 towers and four gateways (three survive). The rise in the road level (approx 1.5m over the centuries) robs magnificent gateway – **Pends**, Pends Road, 14th century – of its soaring proportions. The other two gateways – **Teind's Yett**, Abbey Walk, with its great arch to accommodate wagons, and the **Sea Yett**, Shore, with machicolated bartizan – date from the 16th century.

St Andrews' Castle (Colour plate C5), c.1200 Rugged ruins on strategic clifftop site, strengthened by man-made ditch (as at Ravenscraig Castle). For 400 years wars and sieges, by land and sea, wreaked destruction on this episcopal palace, fortress and state prison. By 1645, the Town Council gave the *coup de grace* and allowed its stones to be used to repair the harbour. In 1801 the sea claimed the three-storey east range and with it the massive circular south-east blockhouse. Nevertheless, for the military historian, it still provides a fund of information; Mine and Countermine, 1546-7, is a rare example of medieval siege techniques and for the sensation-seeker its Bottle Dungeon offers the ultimate incarceration. Although there is still evidence of 13th- and 14th-century work, what survives dates mainly from the 16th century. The 16th-century square foretower, built on late-14th-century heavily revetted base, has a parapet walk supported on distinctive chequered corbels. West is the handsome range containing the corbelled entry – with stylish trappings, 1555. Where blockhouses once menaced, fragmented curtain walls run north, to the north-west Sea Tower (containing the Bottle Dungeon) and to the north-east Kitchen Tower with its slop sink and garderobe chutes.

University
Although the university buildings are now located throughout the town three colleges have the lion's share of the best architecture.

College of St Salvator, North Street (after a period of decline it was combined in 1747 with the College of St Leonard and became known as the **United College of St Salvator and St Leonard**). On the street front the **Collegiate Church**, the dramatic **Gate Tower** and the plain **Tenement**, 75 North Street, to the west, all date from 1450-60. Of the original magnificent church only the much-buttressed

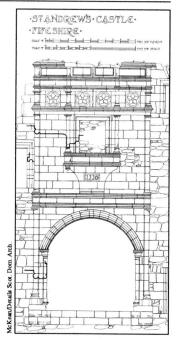

1558 Triumphal arch entrance to St Andrews' Castle, showing an early interpretation of classical motifs

Bishop Kennedy's 1458 tomb in St Salvator's

Top *St Salvator's Collegiate Church, as drawn by Billings c.1847.* Above *Entrance*

shell of the nave and three-sided apse remain. Vaulted roof was replaced by timber in 1773, an operation which severely damaged Bishop Kennedy's tomb, 1458 (said to be the finest example of medieval craftsmanship in Britain). Window tracery and buttress pinnacles were provided in 1861-3 by Robert Matheson. The superb gateway, late 15th century, containing founder's arms, was rebuilt on this site in 1906. Internal refurnishing in 1928-31 was by Reginald Fairlie.

The tower and spire (two tiers of lucarnes) c.1550, has a total height of almost 38m, the highest spire in St Andrews. Through its base is the vaulted gateway to the College. The first floor of the west block (top storey and back wing, 1683-90) contains the notable, panelled Hebdomadar's Room.

Behind the church the original cloister court and buildings have been demolished and the enlarged gracious quadrangle is bounded on the south by semi-elliptical arched **Cloister**, 1848, William Nixon, and on the east and north by **College Buildings**, designed in Jacobean style by Robert Reid, Government architect. His north section of the east range was extended south in the same style by Gillespie & Scott in 1904-6. In the north range, 1845-6, William Nixon modified his predecessor's design and included the well-proportioned College Halls.

College of St Leonard
Off the Pends Road, the main relic of this 249College is its church, now **St Leonard's Chapel** (originally, c.1413, Parish Church of St Leonard). Reconstructed, using 12th-century masonry, in the early 16th century when it became part of the College (1512), with choir for college use and nave for parochial services. The square-headed, 'perpendicular' mullioned windows date from that period. West tower and college buildings adjoining (built c.1540), and enclosing buildings at the east and west ends (built c.1600), have all been demolished. The choir contains three fascinating Early Renaissance mural monuments, 1586-1630, After the 'uniting' of the Colleges in 1747 and transfer of the congregation to St Salvator's Church in 1761, the roof and the west tower (c.1540) were demolished. Re-roofed in 1910, and completely renovated in 1948-52 by I G Lindsay.

The other relic of the College is the 250**Residential Range** of 10 small two-storeyed units: east, five (1617), west, five (1655). Much of its plain architecture disappeared when it was divided into two houses. **St Leonard's West** (acquired *c.*1800), which was given a pedimented north addition with crenellated parapet and a south bow; **St Leonard's East** (reconstructed 1852-4, John Milne), which included a large north addition in Tudor style. Both are now part of **St Leonard's School** where, on the west ⁵¹range, Gillespie & Scott's ogee-roofed **tower**, 1900, contributes to St Andrews' skyline.

Top *Tomb in St Leonard's.* Left *College of St Mary – a peaceful quadrangle .* Above *St Leonard's Chapel*

College of St Mary, South Street
⁵²**Principal's House**, 1539-41, Walter Marr, Master of Works
The first-floor windows have shafted surrounds and contain a striking representation of the Royal Arms of Scotland. The main features on the quadrangle side are the Founder's Tower with prominently corbelled belfry (normally festooned with doves) and, at the re-entrant of the Principal's House, the entrance Stair Tower with notable ogee-roof. Between the two towers

Bishop James Kennedy, founder of College of St Salvator, 1450, was a grandson of Robert III and former Chancellor of Scotland. He was described *'wondrous godlie and wise, weill learned in devine services, and in the civill lawis'.* It was his niece, Kate, which gives her name to the colourful Kate Kennedy Pageant in which, annually, male students process the streets depicting characters associated with 'Town and Gown' from St Andrew to the present day. Kate herself is impersonated by a beardless bejant (a first-year student).

Top *The University Library, South Street.* Above *The University Library, north façade*

South Street in 1926 by Malcolm Patterson

is a magnificent three-storey range with finely carved embellishments. The wing to the south is less ornate. Inside a beautiful prayerhall and an original student's room are preserved.

253 **The University Library**, South Street, 1612-43 Originally consisted of ground-floor 'Public School' sometimes known as Parliament Hall (Scottish Estates met there in 1645-6) and library on first floor. Remodelling (including raising height of upper storey), 1764-7, designed by John Gairdner, provided the austere classical façade of slightly projecting pedimented bays alternating with key-blocked niches. (In 1829-30 Robert Reid continued the same design in his extension west and formed the obelisked gateway to the quadrangle.) Gairdner's elegant **Upper Hall** is galleried with Doric columns. The adjoining **Senate Room**, 1830, Robert Reid, was modified in 1905 by Rowand Anderson, who preserved the handsome proportions of the original.

254 The **Library** expanded south to complete the east side of the picturesque quadrangle. Enormous holm oak dominates. The more modest hawthorn tree is said to have been planted by Mary, Queen of Scots. The first library extension, 1889-90, W W Robertson, took the form of a galleried hall in Scots Renaissance style. In 1908, Sir Robert Lorimer added a balustraded wing in Petit Trianon style (internally bookstacks were of steel with glass floors). A final wing, comparatively plain, was designed 1959 by Reginald Fairlie & Partners. In the 1970s mansard roofs conceal extensive reconstruction to accommodate the Psychology Department, Walker & Pride.

In the garden south of St Mary's College are the 255 **Bute Medical Building**, 1897-9, Jacobean with prominent curved gables, and the **Bell Pettigrew Museum**, 1907-9; both buildings (by Gillespie & Scott) are now completely reconstructed and extended.

The limits of old St Andrews can be defined by the three 'gaits' – South Street, North Street and Market Street (and their cross wynds) – which extend, slightly diverging, westwards from the Cathedral to their respective ports (of which only the West Port remains). These ports or town gates were customs barriers rather than defensive gates. **South Street** displays the breadth of vision of the medieval planners.

Wishart

In 1412, Henry Wardlaw, Bishop of St Andrews, granted university privileges to a school of higher study started in 1410. It received university status with power to grant degrees, when Papal Bulls were issued in 1413 – the first university founded in Scotland, and in England only Oxford and Cambridge are older. The first buildings, from 1415, associated with the university were the Chapel and 'College' of St John the Evangelist. In 1430, on a site adjacent to St John's, the Pedagogy was founded by Bishop Wardlaw. By 1538, the Pedagogy had been replaced by the **College of St Mary**, founded 1537, and the St John's site was occupied in 1612 by the University Library and 'Public School'. Meanwhile, the other two original colleges had been established: the **College of St Salvator**, founded 1450, by Bishop James Kennedy and the **College of St Leonard**, founded in 1512, by Archbishop Alexander Stewart and Prior John Hepburn.

56 **West Port**, 1589 (*above*)
The best extant example in Scotland, modelled on Netherbow Port, Edinburgh. Central archway flanked by semi-octagonal 'rownds' and 'battling' is supported on chequered corbelling and pierced by neat moulded openings. Side arches, and relief panels (west – David I; east – City Arms) were added during 1843-5 reconstruction.

57 On south side of **South Street No 166**, vignette of 18th-century dwelling small-scale, pantiled, whitewashed with stone margins featuring pend and forestair, reconstructed 1955-7, Gillespie & Scott. **Nos 142-8**, 18th century (reconstructed 1939-1949), by J C Cunningham contains low pend which leads to close along which archetypal 'rig development' took place – **Nos 1-4 Louden's Close** which have been carefully restored. The same arrangement can be found at the adjoining **Alison's Close**, 19th century, while at **Imrie's Close** is the **First Sessions (Burgher) Kirk**, 1749-74 (now a dwelling), reverting again to small scale, pantiles and crowsteps.

58 **Madras College**, 1832-4, William Burn
Designed on a grand scale, Georgian in outline,

Madras College – 'where hooded friars chanted'

Wishart

Jacobean in detail, the main block (with its giant first floor) has bayed windows with distinctive curved gablets and gabled single-storey wings enclosing a heavily arcaded quadrangle. Part of original, the matching Masters' Houses (east and west) define a forecourt of enviable space around 1525 north transept, all that remains of 259**Blackfriar's Church** of Dominican Convent.

Southgait Hall (former Royal Hotel), 1857, 260George Rae displays rococo surrounds at first-floor windows. Behind iron-columned shop at **No 1**, *c*.1800, is pantiled **141**(in Burgher Close), early 18th century (renovated 1964). It has traditionally irregular fenestration in ochre-washed walls, characteristic forestair, pend and porch with masonic symbols. **Nos 109-121** South 261Street, Albert Buildings, 1844, William Scott's civic classicism imported from Dundee.

County Library, Church Square, 1790 262Built as school, the well-proportioned façade of Robert Balfour, 1811, has outlasted all internal transformations.

Top *Blackfriars Church with north frontage of Madras College beyond.* Above and right *Holy Trinity*

263**Holy Trinity**, South Street
Founded by Bishop Wardlaw in 1410-12, only the tower (with stair jamb), two west arches and some piers remain. In the 16th century both tower and jamb acquired spires.

The present 'Toon Kirk' is virtually an original composition in a medieval theme (the crowning achievement of MacGregor Chalmers, 1907-9) in which he distilled his profound knowledge of Scottish church architecture. Two features of the inspiring interior are the magnificent pulpit and the wealth of stained-glass windows by the Strachans, William Wilson, Herbert Hendrie and others. In the south transept is the striking black and white marble **Monument to Archbishop Sharp**, carved in Holland, *c.*1679.

Left *St Andrews' Town Hall and Queen's Gardens.* Above *The Toon Kirk's 15th-century spire*

54 Town Hall, South Street and Queen's Gardens, 1858-62, J Anderson Hamilton
Dominating the centre of South Street, the scale of its mullioned and transomed elevations befits civic importance and the arresting corbelled angle turret displays the St Andrews and Madras College coats of arms. Appropriately, a panel dated 1565, from the Old Tolbooth (Market Street, demolished 1866), has been inset in the hallway.

Queen's Gardens, *c.*1860
The terrace houses on the east side enjoy their

James Sharp (1618-79), wheeler and dealer in 17th-century Church politics. His life touched many places in Fife. In 1648 he was appointed Minister of Crail: by 1661 he was consecrated Archbishop of St Andrews and occupied, as his palace, St Andrews Castle. He acquired Scotscraig in 1667 and Strathyrum in 1669. His overnight stay at Melville Manse, Anstruther and his halts at Kennoway and Ceres on the way to his fate at Magus Muir in 1679 are well documented as is also the deed itself on the pyramid-shaped monument on the Muir and the Greek and Italian marble monument in Holy Trinity Church, St Andrews. Records confirm that on the night before the murder his daughter Margaret stayed at the Castle, Elie.

David Rhind, 1808-83, Edinburgh architect was noted for his Renaissance palazzo style of bank buildings e.g. the opulent Commercial Bank, Gordon Street, Glasgow (1853-7) (now Royal Bank of Scotland). In comparison No 2 Queen's Gardens, St Andrews, is very small fry indeed.

Top *Statue of St Andrew overlooks Church Street from "Citizen' office.*
Above *St John's House, South Street*

amenity gardens on the west; **No 2**, Burgh Offices (former Commercial Bank), 1869, David Rhind, and **No 3**, 1860, William Scott, possess classical individuality but the rest conform to George Rae's master plan.

265 **St Regulus Hall**, 1864-5, George Rae
Steep-gabled and turreted, it provides emphatic southern terminal to the terrace.

266 **St Andrew Episcopal Church**,
Queen's Terrace, 1867-9, Rowand Anderson
Very correct Gothic conceals an interior of Byzantine inspiration. For structural reasons tower, 1892, had to be reduced in height in 1938.

On the corner of **Church Street** the plain
267 tenement, **105 South Street**, c.1800, was reconstructed in Arts & Crafts style to form Citizen Office, 1932, by Walker & Pride. **No 71 South Street**, c.1600 (reconstructed c.1800 when four-columned doorway added), and **Nos**
268 **67-69, St John's House**, c.1450 (reconstructed c.1600, 18th century, 19th century, 1967-75 by W Murray Jack) another group belonging to the University, makes an impressive contribution to
269 the street architecture. **Nos 44-62**, 16th/17th century, a notable series of mansions with a subtle curve as a building line. Built for prosperous burgesses some still retain 16th-century vaulted cellars and most have their *lang rigg* garden walls (almost 200m long) as recorded in 1567 disposition. Latterly Georgian features appear and **No 46**, remodelled 1723, has impressive classical façade – corbelled parapet, V-jointed pilaster end-strips and Doric-columned doorway with arms of the one-time owner, Principal Haddow.
270   The harled street frontages identify **South Court**, 40-42 South Street, and the **Great Eastern**, 36-38 South Street (both 16th century), which were flatted in 1968-72 by W Murray Jack. They retain arms of their one-time owners George Martine, c.1660, and Prior Hepburn, c.1521, respectively. Note the late-16th-century arcade (revealed in the courtyard during the reconstruction) and against the plain 17th-century south gable a curious rubble lean-to with classical detailing.
271   **No 24 South Street**, late 17th century, was imaginatively restored in 1970-1 by W Murray Jack. Round the corner in tranquil setting of **St Leonard's Lane** an exquisite Georgian doorway can be seen.

Above *Deans Court with University motto and crest above doorway.* Left *Queen Mary's House, Garden frontage*

72 Queen Mary's House, South Street, *c*.1525
A plain street elevation gives no hint of the romantic improvisations of the garden front. On a south gable, an elaborate corner oriel projects from a fine panelled room traditionally associated with Mary, Queen of Scots. An early-17th-century crowstepped lean-to barely clears the oriel. At the main re-entrant angle a splayed stairtower rises, corbels to the square, and terminates in a crowstepped caphouse. Adjacent, and boldly scribed to splay and corbel, is a fine pedimented early-18th-century porch. Opposite are the excellent stone frontages of **Nos 1-7 South Street** especially the distinctive corner 73 tower at **No 1, the Roundel**, 16th century.

74 **Deans Court** (opposite Cathedral) is *the oldest dwelling on the oldest domestic site in St Andrews*. It is suggested that its vaulted core was part of the first archdeacon's house of the 12th century. The present L-plan was repaired by Sir George Douglas, *c*.1585 (his arms above gateway). It was divided into two houses (*c*.1730) then Victorianised (Baronial version) in 1876. De-Victorianised in 1950-1 by Walker & Pride, and converted and enlarged into University residence. Restoration of many original features

The practise of photography was first established in Scotland in St Andrews, immediately after the announcement of the invention of the Calotype process by W H Fox Talbot in 1840, and the locality features prominently in early photographs as a result of the work of a group of scientists. Prominent among them was Dr John Adamson, who resided for many years in South Street (the Post Office building bears a commemorative plaque). Together with his younger brother Robert (who subsequently formed an important but tragically brief photographic partnership with the painter, lithographer and RSA Secretary David Octavius Hill) and others including Sir David Brewster (inventor of the kaleidoscope and one time Principal of the United Colleges of St Salvator and St Leonard) and Thomas Rodger. Dr Adamson pioneered the development of the Calotype process in Scotland, producing his first such print in 1841. Thomas Rodger opened the first photographic studio in St Andrews in 1848 and, some years later, built larger studio premises in St Mary's Place which now house the University Careers Advisory Service.

included rehabilitation of vaulted lower floors and panelled rooms. Fine courtyard with draw-well and mature walled garden, complete a memorable property.

North Street is largely spared commercial disfigurement. The old fishing quarter was at its east end where small traditional houses still 275exist. **Nos 12-16**(now museum) and **Nos 18-20**, early 18th century, both carefully reconstructed in 1938 by James Scott. Round corner in **South** 276**Castle Street, No 11**, c.1700, restored 1961; **Nos 13-15**, 1735, restored 1964, retain their 277forestairs. **Nos 19-21** North Street, 17th/18th century, have the only example of pillared forestair left in St Andrews. In cobbled setting of 278**North Castle Street, Nos 35-39**, 17th and 18th century, **No 41**, 18th century, and **No 43**, rebuilt late 18th century, all retain a flavour of old St 279Andrews. **All Saints Episcopal Church Buildings**, North Castle Street and North Street, offer a variety of styles. Elevated Gothic chancel and pyramid-capped bell tower, 1906-9, John Douglas; nave (barrel-vaulted) and delightful entrance court with Doric loggia, 1919-24, Paul Waterhouse. North side of the court, **Castle Wynd House** is 17th-century vernacular with five-storey V-fronted tower, 1921, Paul Waterhouse. North Street frontage Reginald Fairlie's pantiled **Rectory**, 1937-8, in 17th-century Scots idiom planned around a courtyard.

280**Younger Graduation Hall**, 1923-9, Paul Waterhouse
Although gifted to the University by Dr James Younger of Mount Melville, its alien giant neoclassical style made conservationists fume. Now, some claim familiarity has made an 'eyesore' into an oddity. The excellent **No 77**

Top left *12-16 North Street*. Top right *Detail of Admiral Fitzroy's Barometer, North Street*. Above *North Street in 1926 by Malcolm Patterson*

Left *Younger Graduation Hall.*
Above *Forestair on College Street.*

31North Street (Old Students' Union), 16th century remodelled late 18th century; it is three-storey with prominent semicircular stairtower (mid-16th century), raised through its original oversailing roof, 1923-4, by Paul Waterhouse.

32Crawford Arts Centre, North Street, has as its centrepiece the scholarly Adam-style house, c.1812, built as town residence of the Lindsays of Wormiston. The original winged composition included forecourt flanked by simple detached single-storey buildings, now somewhat altered.

Below *Crawford Arts Centre.* Left *University Library*

3University Library, 1972-6, Faulkner-Brown, Hendy, Watkinson, Stonor

A massive multi-tier sandwich of concrete and smoked glass.

Market Street
The shape of the main street, which roughly bisects the area between North and South Streets, recalls a historic role as community centre of the burgh. The Mercat Cross and Tron stood at the intersection of College and Church Streets. The west end of Mercat Place was defined by the Tolbooth, 1565, demolished 1866, which was situated centrally where the street narrows opposite Muttoes Lane. The narrowing of Market Street beside the Union Street junction marks the east end of Mercat Place. Most of the buildings are Victorian. All that 284remains of the early architecture are **No 88**, late 18th century, three-storey tenement with central bays raised impressively to four storeys and 285pedimented and **No 68**, with narrow crowstepped gable, renovated 1950, T P Rodger.
286 **Cross Keys**, *c.*1850, George Rae, is a former hotel, now flatted. Good late-Georgian example with freer treatment on east addition, 1864. **Nos** 287**77-79** Market Street, 1852, George Rae, whose 288office was on first floor. **Mercat House**, 1 Church Street, 1873, John Milne, is a monumental Scottish Baronial corner block.

Church Street
After the 19th-century cast-iron columned shop fronts at **Nos 8,9** and **21**, the refurbishment for 289the **Trustee Savings Bank** in 1989, including glass and iron à la Charles Rennie Mackintosh, gained the Nicoll Russell Studio an RIBA Award.

St Andrews Harbour (Colour page C5)
On the estuary of Kinness Burn it dates from 13th century. Although often repaired, renewed and occasionally extended, it retains its medieval form. The main pier – the traditional after-Sunday service walk of the red-gowned students – was rebuilt in stone taken from the Cathedral in 1656. The cross-pier and inner harbour were formed in the early 19th century. 290The harled and pantiled **Bell Rock House, Shorehead** (former tavern), late 18th century, is the last survivor of picturesque buildings which once lined the harbour. Round the cliffs 291from the harbour, **Kirkhill**, East Scores, 1973-4, Walker & Pride, a housing development on sensitive site, uses traditional forms and materials adapted to modern needs.

The Scores, between cliff edge and the Old Town, began to develop in the second half of the 19th century. **Castlecliffe**, 1869, David Bryce, confirms his training under William Burn, i.e. good plan clad in asymmetric Baronial style. Detailing relatively modest compared with George Rae's profusion at **Edgecliffe**, 1864-6. **Swallowgate**, 1894-5, Rowand Anderson, shows some lighter touches, e.g. ogee-roofed bays. All these private mansions are now part of the University. One purpose-made University residence on The Scores is **St Salvator's Hall**, 1927-30, extended in 1937-40 by Mills & Shepherd – Oxbridge Gothic.

St James Church, The Scores, 1909-10, Reginald Fairlie
Although on cliff-edge his first independent commission looks compact and safe with squat tower and bellcast roofs.

Off Abbey Walk lie the St Leonard's School residences of **St Nicholas House**, 1930, Reginald Fairlie, in muted Scots Renaissance. **Abbey Park House** is late 18th century, once a handsome Georgian residence in spacious landscaped setting.

New Town St Andrews had a fragmented start e.g. **Nos 79-81 North Street**, 1824-5, Balfour Robert, and **No 150**, early 19th century, attributed to George Rae. But George Rae, under the enthusiastic patronage of Provost Hugh Lyon Playfair, began to transform the medieval town. North Bell Street (now **Greyfriar's Gardens**) and (South) **Bell Street** were planned, **Queen's Gardens** followed (see p.127). All made valuable contributions to Georgian St

Top *Greyfriars Gardens*. Centre *St James Church*. Below *Abbotsford Crescent*

Andrews. **Playfair Terrace, Nos 1-8**, 1846-52, George Rae, is an excellent symmetrical classical design with strong horizontal channelling on ground floor. The middle block, **Nos 4** and **5**, is raised and gabled with palmette finials. The later porch at **No 1** and the dormer at **No 8** are eyesores. **Lockhart Place, Nos 1-4**, 1847, George Rae, implemented by others, reveals a more delicate touch. On The Scores, **Gillespie Terrace**, 1850, master-planned by George Rae, but subsequently modified, includes the non-classical twin-bowed **No 2**. The undisputed heart of the New Town has three geometric components – the straight terrace **Nos 1-14 Hope Street**, 1847; the convex curve **Nos 1-15 Howard Place**, 1860s; and the concave curve of **Nos 1-13 Abbotsford Crescent**, 1865, John Chesser – ordered civic planning in the classical style. Continuity is

achieved by fenestration, cornices and string-courses supplemented by railings and fly-over entrance steps. Emphasis occurs at the doorways: consoled at **No 15 Howard Place**, and Ionic portico at **Abbotsford House**, 1869.

In the wake of these stylish terraces are the 305dinosaurs of the 19th century: **Royal & Ancient Club House**, 1854, single storey by George Rae inflated into overblown Victorianism; and 306**Hamilton Hall**, 1895, J M Munro, in red Dumfries stone and equally alien dome.

Rusacks Marine Hotel,
1886-7 and 1891, D Henry
Redeemed by its exciting six-storey pediment front on Pilmour Links. Their 20th-century counterparts include **The Old Course Hotel**, off Guardbridge Road, 1967-8, Curtis & Davis, whose monolith of bay and balcony aroused public protest; subsequent costly reconstructions 1982-90 now package the golfers' luxury in, appropriately, 'Sunningdale Stockbroker' style 307and **Golf Museum**, Golf Place, 1990, Hurd Rolland which was half-buried to appease the preservation lobby; exposed elevations with viewing platform suggests 'Red Square monumental'; inside, a multi-media display.

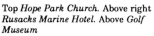

Top *Hope Park Church*. Above right *Rusacks Marine Hotel*. Above *Golf Museum*

308**Hope Park Church**, 1864-5, Peddie & Kinnear
An early geometric style expressed in hammer-dressed masonry. Like all St Andrews land-

marks its sharp-pointed steeple provides vital direction for golfers on the links. Across the [09]road, Renaissance-detailed **Nos 3-6 Alexandra Place** (former Station Hotel), 1869-70, Jesse Hall, converges on a sturdy corner tower in which are lodged segmental-headed dormers.

[10]**Volunteer Hall**, Alexandra Place, 1884, Hall & Henry
Early utilitarian example of structural ironwork with elliptical trusses leaving clear floor area of [11]30 x 15m. **Gibson House**, Argyle Street, 1882-4, Hall & Henry, is symmetrical Jacobean, with classical decoration on ogival-roofed tower.
[12]**Argyle Court**, Argyle Street, 1986, James F Stephen, is a brave attempt to bring the vernacular into the 20th century. **Kinburn House**, Double Dykes Road, 1856, by John Milne is Georgian with mock fortifications.

Kennedy Gardens provides more contrasting examples of John Milne's mansions: **Rathmore**, 1861, a break from tradition in bizarre Gothic, and **Wardlaw Hall** (former Westerlea), 1865-8, top-heavy Scots Baronial. Both overlook **North Haugh**, the site of the mid-20th century expansion of the University. In their various forms, the **Physics** (1965), **Mathematics** (1967) and **Chemistry** (1968) Buildings, William Holford & Associates, solved clamant accommodation problems, but failed to acknowledge tradition.

Andrew Melville Hall, 1964-8, James Stirling
The North Haugh Campus could be anywhere

Left *Andrew Melville Hall.* Top *Argyle Court.* Above *Rathmore, Kennedy Gardens*

Westerlea, Kennedy Gardens, received an Honourable Mention in the 1874 International Exhibition of Architecture.

and this exercise in precast concrete units did nothing to dispel the illusion.

Top *Wayside – now sub-divided. Main gable is now principle feature of Wayside Easter.* Top right *St Leonard's Parish Church.* Above *Law Mill at Lade Braes*

St Leonard's Parish Church,
1902-4, P MacGregor Chalmers
An essay in neo-Romanesque by the acknowledged expert. Simple nave, west aisle, and apses formed in excellent stonework and enhanced by good stained glass. Tower, unusually, is not spired but gable-roofed.

Wayside, 98 Hepburn Gardens,
1901-4, Robert Lorimer
His Scottish Lutyens role. South front features typical cusped gable and dormer. Textures of stone and slate (in plain and undulating roofs) blend harmoniously.

North-West of St Andrews, off A91
The earliest port of St Andrews was on the Eden Estuary. The route to the Royal Burgh lay across the bleak links to the famous **Swilken Bridge**, 17th/18th century. Traditionally low parapets accommodated pack ponies.

313 Strathtyrum, from 1720-40
A remote mansion hidden by dense woods, once the haunt of many famous literary figures, when rented to John Blackwood, publisher. Original house, 1720-40, lies to the north-west, and is roughcast with pedimented centre jamb. In front is Robert Balfour's impressive nine-bay block, c.1805, on raised basement, where (on the south-east frontage) broad fly-over steps mount to a lofty semicircular portico – which protects the fine fanlit doorway in the pedimented centre. **Stable block**, 1817, is a U-plan with pedimented gables while **mausoleum**, 1781, exhibits an eccentric Gothic style. By the urn-

Arts in Fife

capped swagged **gate piers**, early 19th century,
the small **lodge**, 1821, features a pedimented
Doric porch.

West of St Andrews
14 **Denbrae** and **Dewar's Mills**, 17th/18th
centuries, are a picturesque group of traditional
buildings becoming ruinous.

Wishart

15 **Clatto**, remodelled by David Bryce, c.1845-50,
John Milne, Clerk of Works. Simplified and
tamed Walker & Pride, 1964.

South-West of St Andrews
Scotland's first public country park, **Craigtoun**,
was formed in the spacious mature-wooded
Mount Melville, home of the Melvilles and
latterly the Youngers, brewers from Alloa. The
architect for all 20th-century work at Mount
Melville (for Dr James Younger) was Paul
16 Waterhouse, his son-in-law. The **Mansion**,
1902-3, is a vast pink sandstone edifice with
small-paned windows. Encouraged by generous
budget, the architect drew inspiration from
many sources to clad classical form. Now a
hospital, modern additions and metal fire-
escapes envelop the original house. As preludes
to **Cypress Avenue**, 18th-century **archway**
(with eagle and urn finials) and 19th-century
gateway with more urn finials. **Dutch Village**,
c.1920, on islet is fantasy in stone, whitewash
and red-tile with fairy-tale turrets and baroque
boat-house. Feature of **walled garden** is the
faceted-roof **summerhouse**, 1902, set in the
wall. **Mount Melville House** (former stable
block), c.1905 – a frontage with steep-pitched

Wishart

Top *Strathtyrum.* Centre *Dewar's
Mill.* Above *Craigtoun Mansion
House (now an hospital)*

Dunino Church in its woodland setting

pavilion roof and angle, square turrets – recalls a French château. Behind is a quadrangular plan with 16th-century Scottish overlay. **West Lodge**, early 20th century, is mini-Baronial. In comparison, **East Lodge**, c.1820, is refreshingly uncluttered and includes semi-octagonal Doric [317]porch. **Greigston Farmhouse**, early/mid 18th-century, betrays superior origins. Advanced single-storey wings (part 'improved') have finials and skewputt busts which overlook forecourt. Entrance door enclosed by Victorian porch. The east end of west range of **steading** (probably part of 17th-century house) has barrel-vault repointed in 1815.

South of St Andrews, off A915
[318]**Priorletham Smithy**, c.1850, is Jacobean with steep-pitched gables and stepped skews.
[319]**Cameron Church**, 1808, is unpretentious Georgian with delicate window tracery and [320]sprightly curved roof on belfry. **Carngour Farmhouse**, c.1860, illustrates when the severity of early Georgian was replaced by 'Jacobethan' – broad eaves, fancy bargeboards with pendants, Tudor hoodmoulds, angled entrance porch.

Dunino Church, 1826-7, J Gillespie Graham Small but sublime Gothic in rural setting. In 1928 the nave with deepset Y-tracery windows acquired a chancel and porch by Waddell & Young (based on MacGregor Chalmers' 1908 design) and the interior, remodelled in natural stone and timber, was enhanced by good stained-glass windows. The **Manse**, 1819, [321]retains its original charm. **Pittarthie Castle**, c.1580, Monypenny of Pitmilly, was remodelled 1682 by William Bruce of Pittarthie. Sited on bleak uplands the L-plan shell with stair tower at re-entrant resembles Randerston (see p.142). Unusual features include shot-holes at window breasts and late 17th century slightly corbelled stair on north elevation.

South-East of St Andrews, off A918
Everyone who climbs the Brownhills Brae turns and feasts their eyes on yet another magnificent view of St Andrews' sea-washed promontory, the Bay, the Angus coastline and the Grampians.

BOARHILLS
A pretty backwater, a comfortable village [322]community. **Boarhills Church**, 1866-7, George Rae, is sturdy and plain. Gothic windows have

simple Y-tracery. The single conceit is its tall, arched belfry with corbelled members. **Parish School**, 1815, of befitting simplicity (before extensions) with single-storey classroom and two-storey master's house under the same roof.

Kenly Green

323**Kenly Green**, *c*.1790

An architectural delight. It seems no coincidence that the north-west parapet of the contemporary **Kenly Bridge**, 1793, develops neatly into its parkwall and entrance gateway. The five-bay main block is finished in white stucco outlined and punctuated with channelled full-height pilasters crowned with urns. The pedimented single-storey pavilions, also urn finialed, continue the theme and the short, set-back links have acceptable 20th-century elliptical windows. **Kenly Green Doocot**, 17th century, restored 1987, has an unusual gable roof (ball-finialed) with swept-dormer, pigeon entrance. Upstream in the Kenly Burn, in a wooded gorge, is the historic **Peekie Bridge**, early 16th century, bearing, on the north side, Hepburn Arms. Many farms still have relics of earlier times, especially arched cartsheds. Contrasting designs of 24 horsemills can be seen at **Bonnytown** (slated 25 conical roof on round plan) and **Falside** (faceted pantile roof on octagonal plan).

Above *Cove Wynd, Pittenweem.*
Right *Kingsbarns Parish Church*

East Neuk

The main strand of the *'fringe of gold'* of the *'beggar's mantle'* (as James VI described this part of Fife) is the coast road from St Andrews to Lundin Links. But, just as farmers claim that land on the seaward side is more fertile and yields the early crop, so, in most towns and villages in the East Neuk, it is in the 'gaits' and wynds, which lead down to the sea, that the best traditional buildings can be found.

KINGSBARNS

The 'barns' which supplied grain to the Royal palaces at Crail and Falkland no longer exist and little remains of the harbour. However, three 'fermtouns' within the village and the surrounding land testify to its historic role.

Parish Church, The Square, c.1630, was radically altered in 1810-11 by Robert Balfour. Plain, but the tower is distinctive. The old base supports later scroll buttresses, while the belfry is deftly broached to octagonal parapet, 1866, George Rae.

The austere **Kingsbarns House**, The Square, 18th century, was reconstructed and extended in 1794 by John Corstorphine (for own use). Architraved entrance with appropriate architects' instruments carved on frieze. Two early 18th-century houses – **Cessneuk** (rubble stone) and **Wellgate** (harled with stone margins) – complete the east side of The Square. Small early 19th-century house (now part of Wellgate) hyphenates the two.

Kingsbarns School, Main Street, 1822
Delightfully eclectic – open pedimented porch,
ogee-capped belfry, round-headed windows with
original glazing. Behind Kingsbarns House,
Grey House, 18th century, elegant with
moulded wallhead, fanlit doorway, and, later,
consoled canopy. Nearby **Monypenny House**
and **Mill House**, both 18th century
(reconstructed 1976), are harled with margins,
to form an attractive group with single-storey
wing and pend arch. **Cambo Arms Hotel**, Main
Street, early 19th century was a Georgian
coaching inn (former stables at rear) its consoled
entrance partly obscured by later porch. **North
Quarter Farm House**, Main Street, is similar,
with all the trimmings – fine doorway and
fanlight in full view.

*Entrance to North Quarter
farmhouse*

*Inscribed scrolled skewputt of the
Old Forge*

Old Forge, North Street, 1799
The delicacy of inscribed scrolled skewputts on
is well worth looking for.

126 **Cambo House**, 1879-81, Wardrop & Reid
For over 300 years the Erskine family has
owned Cambo. The house is ponderous three-
storey Renaissance composition. Entrance bay
pedimented with Ionic order dutifully above
coupled Doric porch. Massive two-storey bays
load the south (garden) front. In contrast, the
stables and **doocot** (octagonal with finialed
parapet), both late 18th century (possibly
contemporary with earlier mansion burned
down in 1878), recall the grace of a previous age.
The **gate lodges**, c.1800, are more monumental
than homely. **Country Park Centre** (former
Easthall Farm), early 19th century
Symmetrical design about a central doocot

Wormston

Balcomie: Below *drawn by*
McGibbon & Ross. Bottom *Gateway*

tower. Distinguished by crenellation treatment and featuring octagonal horse mill (now restaurant).

327 Randerston, late 16th century
Epitome of the laird's house, just about an L-plan. Three storey with a vaulted ground floor. Circular stair-tower at re-entrant is corbelled to rectangular caphouse. Former angle turrets oversailed by roof.

328 Wormiston, 17th century
Dominates Fife Ness, from its thick shelter of trees. Since *c.*1988, the cosily domestic 19th-century additions have all been pulled down. The original dramatic three-storey block and wings have been exposed. Note the old dormerheads (one dated 1629), the rectangular, corbelled stair-tower and its parasitic turnpike.

329 Balcomie, late 16th century
An odd grouping of castle, house and farm. Of the Castle, where Sir James Learmonth received Mary of Guise (second wife of James V), only the west part of four-storey range complete with five-storey tower remains. The original east range now has only a fine, segmental, arched

gateway (with three armorial panels, 1602) standing disconsolately amidst the farm buildings. The west range is mostly Georgian farmhouse, early 19th century, bowed on west front. The south-east part of the walled garden and moulded gateway c.1600, survive.

In 1310, King Robert the Bruce granted the burghers of Crail the right to hold markets on the Sabbath day. For many years after the Reformation the General Assembly of the Church tried in vain to change the market to a weekday.

CRAIL (above)

About 2km short of that *well-aired ancient town* the spire of Crail's kirk comes into view above the trees. Sighting the Firth of Forth and the Isle of May, the traveller knows he or she is approaching the eastern tip of the Fife peninsula. Created a Royal Burgh in 1310, this small, relatively remote, community maintained Royal links. The streets and buildings still reflect one of Scotland's finest historic towns. With decline in fishing, the seasonal holiday makers represent the town's only 'industry'.

At the base of the tower of the Parish Church, deep grooves confirm that medieval archers used its walls to sharpen their steel-tipped arrows. The old Parish Kirkyard was nicknamed the 'Westminster Abbey of Crail' as it contains many family memorials e.g. the mural monuments of the Lumsdens (1598), Bruces (1630) and Moncrieffs (1707).

Left Crail Parish Church

Parish Church, Marketgate, c.1160
This modest Romanesque sapling (nave and chancel) early in the 13th century sprouted side aisles, clerestoreys and free-standing tower

The fish weathervane on the Tolbooth represents the far-famed Crail capon – a haddock, which, some claim, was only sun-dried, others that it was smoked.

Below *Mercat Cross.* Bottom *Golf Hotel.* Below right *The Tolbooth*

(perhaps the oldest in Fife and intended to be one storey higher). Collegiate status in the early 16th century encouraged more growth, enlarged chancel and spire, and by the mid 18th century a multiplicity of lofts. Eventually in 1963, Judith Campbell provided the severe 'pruning' which revealed today's mature, dignified, early Gothic, arcaded design. The treelined **Marketgate** was once one of the largest medieval market places in Europe.

On the north side, the houses are large, built for rich merchants, or as town houses for local

331 lairds. **No 1 Denburn House**(corner sundial dated 1719) incorporates a 17th-century house; both **No 3, Old Manse**, 1789 (second floor added

332 1829, William Lees), and **Kirkmay House**, 1817 (home of the Inglis family), are early classical in

333 style. **No 9, Friars Court,** of rubble stone, dated 1686, is probably Crail's oldest house. **Nos 13-29** are Victorian and John Milne introduced

334 at **Nos 25-29** (1886) contrasting coloured stones, V-plan and bow windows.

South side of Marketgate contains small, vernacular 18th-century houses which retain a certain charm in spite of later insertions of dormers and garages. Note forestairs at **Nos 8** and **36**, marriage-lintels at **Nos 28-30** (1736),

335 and the excellent fore jamb at **Nos 42-44.**

336 **Tolbooth**, Marketgate, 16th century
Most distinctive building in town. Dutch influence on jaunty curves of bellhouse roof is now regarded as tenuous. Upper diminishing stages and roof, 1776 (first built entirely of

wood) are surmounted by 'fish' weathervane.

Adjacent **Town Hall**, 1814, John Corstorphine (altered 1886, John Currie), is unexciting. Chamfered square shaft of nearby **Mercat Cross** dates from early 17th century. **Golf Hotel**, early 18th century, is fashioned to the site. Accent is on corbelled wallhead gable.

At **High Street**, south side, owners have continued to retain traditional character. **Nos 14-16** with **No 2 Castle Street**, 18th century, were renovated by National Trust for Scotland. The **Maltings**, 1960s, at rear of **Nos 55-56**, demonstrate success of sympathetic design even with modern forestairs while **Westgate, Nos 1-6**, shows how conversion into flats can preserve and revitalise 19th-century granary. **No 2, West Green** (c.1850), has Jacobean strapwork decoration and **Nos 20-21** retain 18th-century simplicity.

Shoregate

The oldest road in town links harbour and clifftop: 17th- and 18th-century houses on the right, **Nos 9-11** have interesting gable with moulded doorway; **No 13** resited pediment, 1632; and **No 19** within, door lintel (dated 1613). Steep crowstepped **Custom House, No 35**, late 17th century and **Nos 37-43**, 18th century (round forecourt), all contribute to the harbour scene.

Crail was a settlement by 9th century, a flourishing burgh by late 12th century and was described in James V Charter as *'where sundry princes, his predecessors, had made their residence'*. Among its privileges as a burgh was a monopoly of trade from River Leven round Fife Ness to the Kenly Burn. Crail, however, was always regarded as somewhat remote. One Fife man asked another whether he had been abroad; he replied *'Na, but I ance kent a man who had been to Crail'*.

As at the Pends, St Andrews, the age of the carriageways in Crail is revealed by the relationship of their level to the ground floors of the old buildings. Here, at **Golf Hotel**, there are three steps down at the entrance confirming the rise in carriageway levels of approximately two millimetres per year.

Crail Castle, 12th century, a Royal stronghold and residence of the Constable of Crail originally stood on the clifftop to the east of the harbour. By the 16th century it was ruinous and by 1706 the Town Council proposed redevelopment of the site. Today only its name is recalled in Castle Street and Castle Terrace.

Harbour frontage, Crail

On left side of Shoregate, **No 2**, Burgess House, 18th century, and **No 12**(with **No 25** Castle 343Street) maintain the character. **Castle Terrace,** *c.*1890, without any claims of authenticity, has enough late-18th-century detailing to pass muster. **Nos 22-8**, 17th/18th century, demonstrate part of ageing process which 'moulds' the buildings, their forestairs and their gardens to the steep roadway and the cliff face. 344**No 38**, Harbour Office, terminates the sequence with weathered doorway and forestair.

The Harbour dates from 16th century (when it succeeded natural haven of Roome Bay). At that time, curved breakwater (origin of east pier) was built. Straight stump of the west pier, 1826, Robert Stevenson, originally rubble-built but much repaired. In 1803 it was home for *'6 ships and barks and about 80 fishing boats'*.

28-32 Castle Street (note number plate!)

345**Nos 28-32** Castle Street, 17th/18th century Picturesque vernacular group with 75 Nethergate, with swept dormers and forestairs. **Rumford** comprises a cluster of restored, pantiled, and crowstepped 17th/18th-century dwellings. **Nos 1-2** is dated 1784, **No 7** has 18th-century jamb. **Nos 5-6** was the first rehabilitation work under the National Trust for Scotland's revolving restoration scheme, in 1961, Wheeler & Sproson.

346 **Nethergate,** an 'island' **Library**, 1821-4, former School, Robert Balfour, with Gothic windows; splayed porch, 1852. On south side, **Nos 32-68**, mainly 19th century, all modernised, but still good neighbours with the early 18th 347century at **Nos 36, 38, 68. Nos 18-28 Downie's Terrace,** John Currie, is a curious row in 'rogue' Baronial. **Priory**, 1910, Thoms & Wilkie, is a fashionable essay in Scots Baronial complete with tower and angle turret. **Priory Doocot,** Denburn Park, 16th century, restored 1962, is a

Rumford

cylinder tapered to crenellated parapet.
Nethergate, north side, **Nos 9 to 19**, mid-19th century, well-mannered row, pantiled, rubble-walled, with painted margins. **No 43** (with 8-10 Tolbooth Street) makes attractive corner with splay corbelled to square.

48**Cornceres Farmhouse,** *c.*1840
Quite splendid Scottish Jacobean, steep-gabled L-plan with angle entrance at re-entrant.

49**Airdrie**, 1588, altered 18th century, lies half-way up the 'riggin o' Fife' overlooking the broad coastal plain. Simple, two-storey block of uniform fenestration is overwhelmed by four-storey, south jamb, with round turret. Urned **gate piers**, late 18th century, are, unexpectedly vermiculated. In Fife, doocots (lectern-type), and 50 in ruinous condition, are ten-a-penny; but **West Pitkierie Doocot** (near A950) is a two-storey extravaganza with concave octagonal sides, ball-finialed at angles (Colour page C6).

Doocots. The place of doocots in the life of the Kingdom is enshrined in the definition of a Fife lairdship – '*a wee pickle land, a guid pickle debt, a law plea and a doocot*'. When food was scarce in winter and ice houses rare, doocots were important adjuncts to all landed properties as they provided fresh meat and, not to be overlooked, valuable manure. In 1424, destroyers of doocots were subject to severe penalties and in 1503, parents of children who broke into doocots were fined. In the late Georgian period with agrarian improvements doocots were rendered obsolete – indeed the pigeons became a menace to the crops. The original doocot of 16th century was beehive shaped. In the 17th century the lectern design with pigeon ports half way up the roof slope became common and, of course, there were doocots of special design, either for reasons of aesthetics, or more probably, convenience. Today there still exist in Fife about 100 doocots, most in ruinous condition. Only those of special interest or in good preservation have been noted in this Guide.

Isle of May viewed from above Anstruther

ISLE of MAY
This historic, strategic key to the Forth is 2km long with sheer cliffs 45m high. It became a place of pilgrimage after the Danes murdered St Adrian (*c.*875). David I founded a Priory in the 12th century of which only 13th-century rectangular shell, known as 'The Chapel', survives. **Old Lighthouse**, 1636, John

Kilrenny Parish Church

Innergellie House – garden frontage

Cunningham of Barnes (first in Scotland), now only half of its original height. The **Tower**, 1815-16, Robert Stevenson, in castellated Tudor Gothic still functions, by remote control. **Low Light,** 1844, three-storey round tower plus lantern and single-storey wing – now redundant and used by birdwatchers.

KILRENNY
Once known as Upper Kilrenny as distinct from Lower Kilrenny (now Cellardyke) the village developed under the patronage of the local lairds, the Beatons. Today narrow, twisting streets enjoy the peace brought by the bypass road.

Parish Church, from 15th century
The tower is all that remains of earlier church, used as landmark by fishermen who call it 'St Irnie'. Corbelled parapet and slated spire date from the 16th century whilst the plain church with distinctive obelisk gable finials was built in 1807-8 by Alexander Leslie. In kirkyard **Scott of Balcomie Mausoleum,** *c.*1776, improbable neoclassical design, with inverted saucer-shaped roof; **Beaton Burial Enclosure**, late 17th century, in swagged Ionic order; **Lumsdain's Burial Enclosure,** 1832, effusive classical style adjacent to crowstepped porch, 1932. In Main Street, opposite kirkyard, a typical group of 18th-century dwellings (some modified). Their bright diversity contrasts with grey uniformity of 19th-century education as portrayed by **School House,** 1840, William Lees. **School Room** (now hall), 1815, Robert Taylor & Co. Although individual houses, e.g. late 18th-century **Brownlea Cottage**, Trades Street (gable follows bend in street), catch the eye, the 18th-century plain **Weavers' Cottages** at Tontine Row have more historic significance. **Rennyhill,** *c.*1760, severe three storeys in ashlar, redeemed by key-blocked circular windows in the west gable. Later porch.

351**Innergellie House**, 1740
Exotic flowering of baroque: on the main, north front, Ionic order pervades giant angle pilasters, fluted pilasters at doorway, columned and pedimented panel above. Elsewhere, for good measure, there are key-blocked niches at first-floor level and key-blocked bull's-eyes, with pediments above, at second-floor level. The octagonal Venetian tower at re-entrant acquired top storey in 19th century. The pedimented **East**

Innergellie House. North façade is unusually Baroque

Lodge, late 18th century, presides over rusticated gate piers.

CELLARDYKE

Cellardyke has long basked in obscurity, overshadowed by its neighbour, Anstruther. From the clifftop can be seen the narrow ledge bounded by the seawall and the cliffs where house foundations cling to rocky outcrops. The **Harbour** (once known as Skinfast Haven) dates from 16th century. It was rebuilt, 1829-31, by Joseph Mitchell. Weathered piers and narrow seaway bear testimony to the exposure of the situation at times enlivened when the Shore

The Harbour, Cellardyke

Anstruther's native poet, William Tennant (1784-1848) in due course became Professor of Oriental Languages at St Andrews University – a somewhat elevated step for the author of *Anster Fair*, 1812 – a racy, full-blooded piece with fantastic rhymes. In a more sombre mood but with the same poetic licence he described the outcome of John Knox's rabble-rousing:

'Gaed to Sanct Androis toun
And wi John Calvin in their heads
And hammers in their hands
and spades
Enraged at idols, man and beads
Dang the Cathedral doon.'

Street housewives exercise their right to dry their washing on the quayside.

Shore Street has an 18th-century core, e.g. **Nos 6,7,** and **8** (oriels later), together with **No 12** (note forestair) all retain original features. With the increased prosperity of fishing industry **Nos 14** and **19** acquired additional storeys in the 19th century. **Nos 1** and **2 Harbour Head,** 18th century (recently restored), form an attractive pair while, at the opposite end of the harbour, **Harbour House,** early 19th century, (reconstructed later) with built-in barometer, is exposed but secure. Even the swept dormers look snug. The only original houses to step up the cliff, albeit irregularly, are in **Toft Terrace**, e.g. **No 1,** late 18th century, built direct on the rock and **No 1 Dove Street,** late 18th century, restored by National Trust for Scotland in 1967; high-level braeside garden gives direct access to attic loft. On west side of the **Town Hall,** 1883 by Hall & Henry is the **Kilrenny Cross,** 1642, chamfered square shaft with enriched cap.

Gathering storm over Anstruther Harbour

ANSTRUTHER EASTER

This Burgh of Barony (1572) and Royal Burgh (1580s), lying between Caddys Burn on the east and Dreel Burn on the west, is the central of three burghs: Wester and Easter Anstruther and Cellardyke. *'The nuclear points round which the pattern of each burgh has evolved are the Kirk, the Cross and the Harbour'.*

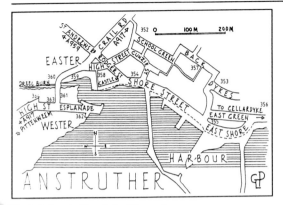

Fragments of Dreel Castle, 1663, can still be found in the wall of Wightman's Wynd. The castle's high and narrow proportions and limited accommodation were reflected in Charles II's comments on having dined in Sir Philip Anstruther's tower room *a fine supper I've gotten in a craw's nest*. Sir Philip, in an attempt to rectify the situation, built a new mansion **Anstruther Place** which was demolished in 1811 to make way for the turnpike road. Dreel Castle was the meeting place of the notorious *Beggars' Benison of Anstruther* secret society – A *Scottish Society of an erotic and convivial nature composed of the Nobility and Gentry of Anstruther* founded 14th September 1739.

52St Adrian's Parish Church,
School Green, 1634
The finialed parapet and spire were added in 1644 and therefore, apart from minor modifications, this church is entirely a product of the 17th century. The high slated roof gives the church a barn-like appearance; the corbelled stages, parapet, and the stair turret of the tower suggest a lopsided telescope. The round-headed window motif is repeated, in doublets on tower, in triplets on south wall of church, and (larger version) on east gable.

Below *No 7 Wightman's Wynd.* Bottom *Doorway in the Esplanade, drawn by A W Webster*

53Chalmers Memorial Church, Backdykes, 1889, David Henry
Abandoned in 1988, this church exhibits Gothic verticality on a prominent site above the harbour.

Castle Street, 17th/18th and 19th century, in spite of some 'improvements', continues to be a genteel terrace. The oldest house is **No 7** with forestair, on corner of Wightman's Wynd.

On **Shore Street** the **Mercat Cross**, 1677, by Andrew Young was re-erected in 1875; yet another chamfered square shaft, this time with corroded iron finial.

Harbour (Colour page C6)
Original pier, perhaps 17th century, which in due course became today's central pier. The West Pier, 1753, became breakwater, and East Pier was formed in 1866-77 by Alan Stevenson and John Hawkshaw. A fitting haven for what was (before 1914) the capital of the winter herring fishing.

Shore Street presents a lively façade to the

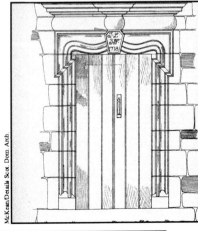

Scottish Fisheries Museum – nets drying in the courtyard

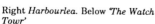

354harbour. **No 7,** Murray Library, 1908, J & T W Currie, is intricate Jacobean in red ashlar; **25-27** are 17th/18th century with elaborately moulded windows; **29-30,** early 19th century classical; **41-44,** 17th century with corbelled stair turret at pend; and **48,** 18th century, with crowstepped street gable. Behind, still with some of the original flavour of the 16th and 17th centuries, are **Tolbooth, Card's** and **Hadfoot Wynds.**

355**Scottish Fisheries Museum,** Harbourhead, 1969-73, W Murray Jack
A creative refurbishment of a motley collection of semi-ruinous buildings around a cobbled courtyard. On the west, an 18th-century ship chandler's house, marriage lintel dated 1721; on the north, mid-19th-century store (the stonehead of double lancet windows of building it replaced – Chapel of St Ayles, demolished 1850 – is incorporated on the south front); the 16th-century Abbot's Lodging (where monks from Balmerino Abbey stayed when they came to buy fish) completes the east side. A saltwater aquarium is provided, a fisherman's dwelling and a wheelhouse have been recreated and fishing nets festoon the 'gallowses' in the courtyard.

Right Harbourlea. Below *'The Watch Towr'*

356**Harbourlea, East Green,** 1981, Baxter Clark & Paul
Competition-winning sheltered housing development on the corner of Burnside Terrace demonstrates that careful modern design can still be sympathetic to the traditional past. Other details catch the eye, e.g. **Nos 27** and **29** late 19th century, pilastered bow shop windows; **26,** 1841, 17th-century carved panel (coopers' tools); **19**(former prison, two cells extant) c.1828, forecourt and forestair. **11-13** were reconstucted in 1968 with style.

357**Old Manse,** Backdykes, 1590
This distinguished building cost its celebrated

Old Manse, Anstruther

Minister,the diarist James Melville, 3500 marks, the parish providing the *'stane and lime'*. On gable of south jamb is panel inscribed *The Watch Towr*. The original three-storey L-plan with corbelled turret-stair at re-entrant became T-plan when the west wing was added in 1753 (restoration 1977-8 by W Murray Jack).

The Revd James Melville who built Melville Manse learned to play golf at school near Montrose and continued to play when a student at St Andrews in 1571 equipping himself with *'bow, arrose, glub and bals'* for his archery and golf.

'58 At west end of High Street, one can meander back in time into the tranquillity of **Old Post Office Close**, 18th century, and Dr Thomas Chalmers' birthplace at **No 3,** crowstepped and pantiled, repaired 1885. **No 24** High Street *c.*1880, a flourish of Victorian Renaissance with pilastered front, curved angles and French-style roof.

'59 **Smugglers Inn**, late 16th century
Profitable but illegal route via Isle of May and the Dreel Burn justified the name of this old coaching inn by the Dreel Bridge. It suffered many 19th-century alterations and additions.
60 **Old Corn Mill**, 1702, top floor 19th century, has attractive massing now smudged by roughcast.

ANSTRUTHER WESTER
Across Dreel Bridge or, at low tide, across the stepping stones in the Dreel Burn, lies Anstruther Wester, Burgh of Barony (1154) and Royal Burgh (1580s).

361 **St Adrian's Church Hall**
(former Parish Church), High Street
Good example of a 16th-century bell tower – a sturdy four storeys and a deep parapet containing slated spire.

St Adrian's Church Tower, Wester Anstruther is said to have been fitted in the 13th century with an iron basket in which a fire was lit to guide the ships approaching the harbour.

The Church (now hall), 1846, James Smith, is
plain with simple Georgian proportions. The
house, 1795, adjacent to tower, was converted to
Town Hall in 1912. The **kirkyard** overlooks
the estuary of the Dreel Burn and fragments of
the 17th-century harbour, ruinous by 1703.

*Anstruther Wester – the Esplanade
with former Parish Church in the
distance*

*Pittenweem Tolbooth and Mercat
Cross*

362**White House,** 1 The Esplanade, 1760
A resplendent cornerpiece with painted margins,
and curvilinear wallhead gable, to a street of
character; **2,** 18th century (former inn, see sheaf
of wheat on sculptured panel); **3,** dated 1718, is
embellished with scroll skewputts and ogee
moulding at doorway; **5,** Old Manse, 1703, has
interesting panels and inscriptions. **High
Street** is mainly 18th century with 19th-century
modifications. Mid-18th-century entrance at **No
43** is worth a look. On corner of north side
363**Buckie House,** 2 High Street, late 17th century
(so called for its gable shell, or buckie, design,
mid-19th century, Andrew Batchelor).

364**Dreel Tavern,** 14-16 High Street,
17th/18th century
Former coaching inn, although modernised,
retains much of original rugged character. **No
18,** late 18th century, features wallhead attic
gable. **No 28,** 1702, parades finely moulded
entrance with lugged architraves, inset
dormerhead, dated 1640, and swept dormers –
marred only by dry dash rendering.

PITTENWEEM (Colour page C7)
Today the busiest fishing port in Fife. Yesterday,
a town of prosperous merchants with a bustling
trade, particularly with the Low Countries.
History marks its status: a port for at least 750
years – Burgh of Barony in the reign of James

View over Pittenweem Harbour from School Wynd with the Isle of May on the horizon

III; Burgh of Regality in 1452; Royal Burgh in 1541. A town of two centres: the Market Place on the clifftop, and the harbour along the water's edge. Linking wynds stagger down steep slopes.

Pittenweem Parish Church

5 **Parish Church**, High Street, from 1588
Although of ancient origin, the church now

basks in the reflected glory of a west tower, 1588, which was the **Tolbooth**. As such it contains traditional vaulted ground floor with council chamber above. Dating from the early 17th century, a projecting fifth storey, containing bell, is crowned by a graceful spire, encircled with coronet-like balustrade. Only the squared terminal of the turnpike breaks the pattern. Traces of early 13th-century work can be detected in the walls of the narrow church, 1532, which was extended to T-plan by north wing, with decorated gable front, in 1882, by James Brown, Session Clerk. **Mercat Cross**, 1736, is on west wall of tower, shaft with egg-and-dart enrichment.

High Street with Kellie Lodging at extreme left and the Tolbooth in the distance

366**Kellie Lodging**, 23 High Street, *c.*1590; restored, 1969-71
Once the town house of Earls of Kellie. Main delight is the fore jamb, chamfered on exposed angles then corbelled out to square, two-storey caphouse, supported on a continuous corbel course which embraces the turret stair at the re-entrant (a detail also seen at Kellie Castle). In the 17th century, wallhead of main block was raised. In this town of steep, bleak wynds the flat spaciousness and the trees of **Market Place** 367are welcome. **Nos 2-3**, 18th century, has forestair and **Nos 6, 7, 8**, *c.*1850, offer a scrolled wallhead chimney. Just visible over the aesthetically disastrous commercial premises is 368the fine wallhead gable of **Nos 34, 36**, 18th century. This links well with **Nos 40** and **42**, 18th, early 19th century, later renovated.

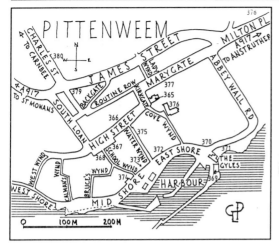

Top *Tangle of the sea.* Above *The Gyles*

Harbour (Colour pages C7 & C8)
Still the hub of local industry, Pittenweem
harbour dates from medieval times and almost
certainly succeeded the 'Boat Haven', the
original tidal jetty off Rockvilla at west end of
Mid Shore, where the fishing boats were
beached. At the harbour the East Pier was first
built in stone, c.1600; West Pier, now in the
centre, built 1724; and finally South Pier in the
19th century. The gaunt three-storey **Fish
Market**, c.1800, now houses 20th-century
utilities.

Gyles Group, 17th/18th century
Presides majestically over the east end of the
harbour – a kind of illuminated capital in soft
red and stark white, to the magnificent line of
Scottish domestic architecture which extends
west along the seafront – the tall 19th-century
terrace on East Shore, the 19th-century houses
on Mid Shore, and the 18th-century assortment
on West Shore. Restored by Wheeler & Sproson
for National Trust for Scotland, 1962.

9 **Gyles House**, 1626
A sea-captain's dwelling, stone margined and
roll-moulded on stair jamb. **No 7**, where sea
gable clings like a limpet to the rocks; **4-6**, 1597,
was rebuilt late 17th century and features a
massive wallhead gable, with stair jamb tucked
under slated lean-to; **3**, dating from the 17th
century, retains original forestair; the oriel is
later. At junction of **East Shore** and **Abbey
Wall Road** the sharp change in direction is
signalled by splayed and corbelled corners at

[370]**Nos 1** and **48** respectively. **No 75, Old Meeting**
[371]**House.** (former Relief Church), 1777, was converted to a house by the National Trust for Scotland in 1974; canted to suit slope and site.

East Shore is impressive. **No 5**, *c*.1820, a neat, Georgian double-house, has lost one of its twin doorways at forestair; **7-8**, mid 19th century, has [372]stepped Jacobean dormerheads; while **18**, *c*.1686, has stately Flemish-style curved, wallhead gable.

[373]**Mid Shore, No 4**, late 18th century, a wallhead gable with Venetian window adds distinction.
[374]**Nos 11** and **12**, 18th century, frontage set back from street with an attractive forecourt. **No 34**, 18th century, retains a pillared forestair.

West Shore (Colour page C8)
The oddly angled, small-scale frontages leave only a narrow passageway between them and the 18th-century tarred rubble seawall. Sunshine makes the bright painted buildings as vivid as Greek island architecture. **Calman's Wynd**, late 18th/early 19th century, painted and pantiled with a forestair in its Gascon's Close branch; **Bruce's Wynd** – 18th century. Gable forestair at **No 17** links with **No 18**. **Water Wynd**, 18th century, perhaps the most interesting; **No 8** with dominant wallhead gable, [375]**No 12**, carefully restored; **No 11** dated 1740, is a gem in dire need of help.

West Shore

St Fillan's Cave, Cove Wynd, alleged retreat of St Fillan, *c*.640, and certainly a place of worship for over 10 centuries. Used for a short time by smugglers it was restored and rededicated in 1935. A natural underground Y-shaped formation it has an altar in one arm and the Saint's Well in the other. A subterranean stair, now sealed at the top, provided unconventional access to the Priory gardens.

Pittenweem Priory
in the late 18th
century by Francis
Grose

McKean/Grose

176 Pittenweem Priory, from 15th century,
Evolved from a foundation of Augustinian
monks who came from the Isle of May in the
13th century. The north-west front of the
gatehouse, 15th century, is dominated by
heavy double-corbelled course, circled to support
'rounds'. The **south-west range** (originally
dormitory and refectory) is in two parts: the
north section, The **Great House**, reformed c.
1588, altered in the 17th century, and features
interesting oriels to courtyard and swept
dormers (perhaps by Sir Robert Lorimer) to Cove
Wynd; the south section, **Town Hall**, 1821, is
now a house, with round-arched windows and
Victorian entrance porch. The **south-east
range**, **Prior's Lodging**, 16th/17th century
(now sub-divided), has been described as
'vaulted ground floor, late-Stewart first floor and
Georgian second floor'.

177 St John the Evangelist Church,
Marygate, 1805
Delicate Gothic, reoriented in 1869-70 when
south chancel moved to east. In 1924 Sir Robert
Lorimer designed fine carvings including pulpit.

178 Christ the King Church, Milton Place, 1830
Classical villa, converted in 1935 to a church.
Sculpture, *Our Lord*, 1952, by Hew Lorimer,
enhances extended porch.

179 No 3 James Street, 1832, has coned-roofed,
canted dormers; while **No 1** (with 5 Charles
Street), c. 1880, sports a bow-fronted shop and
bowed dormers. **Charles Street** (north) is a
street of contrast. **Cosy Cottage**, c. 1800, has
180 quoins and channelled entrance; **No 17** (former

Royal Hotel), *c.*1880, boasts a spectacular three-storey splayed bay, corbelled to square at top. **No 22**, early 19th century, is classical with curved gablet. **Anchor Inn** (former Station Hotel), *c.*1810, embellished with fluted friezes and rosettes, is all presented in black and white.

³⁸¹Balcaskie House, from *c.*1629

Its story is of a native who grew up in the classical tradition and self-conciously assumed a Renaissance dress which, in time, acquired Georgian and Victorian trimmings. Sir William Bruce purchased the laird's tower in 1665 which he enlarged and altered for his own use in 1668-74. In order to create symmetry he extended the original L-plan into a U-plan. The symmetry is approximate since the new crowstepped north wing on the east was broader, and a storey less, than its west counterpart. This disparity is reflected in the four pyramid-roofed, angle-pavilions which pinpointed the new grid layout. The infill between the north wings was raised to three storeys, *c.*1750, and the fine Venetian window placed above the entrance. Additional windows and Jacobean porch, 1830-2, by William Burn, did little to enhance the north elevation. Likewise Burn's iron balcony at first-floor level on the south front, detracts from the simple façade crowned with semi-dormers; and it obscures Bruce's pedimented doorway.

Bruce's symmetric design extended to the grandiose entrance (north) forecourt where service blocks at right angles to the mansion were linked by quadrant screen walls, niched and finialed; and to the garden front where the first large-scale Italian garden in Scotland,

Balcaskie (*above and below*), a *'pretty new house with all modish conveniences of terraces, parks and plantery'*. (Thus Sir Robert Sibbald in 1711, the Fife historian whose uncle owned nearby Gibliston and was able to keep an eye on developments.)

Opposite:
Top *The westernmost acres of the Kingdom.* Middle left *Church of the Most Holy Name, Oakley. Interior with stained glass by Gabriel Loire of Chartres.* Middle right *'The Orient Express'.* Bottom left *Tanhousebrae, Culross.* Bottom right *The Cross, Culross*

Top left *Mercat Cross, Inverkeithing.* Top right *19th century painting of Kirkcaldy.* Middle left *St Fillans Kirk, Aberdour – window depicting arrival of St Colm.* Above *Ravenscraig Castle.* Left *Pan Ha' from Ravenscraig Park*

Top *Hill of Tarvit*. Middle left *Pan Ha', Dysart*. Middle right *Ladybank Pumping Station*. Left *Doocot at Letham Lands*. Above *The Gorge, Dura Den*

C 3

*c.*1670 – focuses on the Bass Rock, 32km distant. The terraces are finely balustraded and boldly buttressed with Roman busts and finials. Much of the work was later remodelled by others, e.g. William Burn, *c.*1826, and W A Nesfield, *c.*1845.

Fortunately, much of Bruce's original interior design remains unscathed, particularly the magnificent painted (de Witt) and plastered (Dunsterfield) ceilings on the first floor, 1674; 19th-century staircases and chimneypieces by Burn and Bryce are worth noting.

Opposite:
Top left *Weathered pillars, St Andrews Cathedral.* Top right *St Andrews Cathedral.* Middle left *Earlshall. Detail of stained glass window.* Middle right *Map of 16th-century St Andrews, showing how original street pattern remains unchanged.* Bottom *View west from Blebo Craigs*

Balcaskie doocots and gate piers at the East Lodge

The most spectacular approach is by the East Drive. The **gate piers**, 1715 (then erected at forecourt of mansion), impress – part rusticated, part fluted, corniced and urn-capped. Furthermore, they are linked by quadrant walls to magnificent twin **doocots**, *c.*1745 – circular, surmounted by conical slate roofs and central birdcages with additional flight holes.

On West Drive is classical **bridge**, 1827, William Burn, with arcaded balustrade and ball-finialed terminal piers.

Carnbee Parish Church, 1793-4, Andrew Horsburgh (wright)
A simple rectangle but birdcage belfry has distinctive, tall pyramid roof. Sir Robert Lorimer designed pulpit and font, pre-1908. He also designed nearby **War Memorial**, *c.*1920, plain shaft bearing shields and cross finial. **Carnbee** is a tranquil hamlet on elevated site overlooking the Forth. **Carnbee House**, former manse, 1819-20, George Dishington, displays all-round classical symmetry. Modern windows have original proportions but bland profile.

²Kellie Castle, 14th century onward
One of the oldest and finest castles in Scotland. Fortunately, fate decreed that first it was abandoned in 19th century and thereby spared

Sir William Bruce (*c.*1630-1710), father of the architectural profession in Scotland and pioneer in planting and garden design. Apart from political activity resulting in a baronetcy his early years saw travel in England and the Low Countries and study of European architecture. In 1665 he bought for his own occupation Balcaskie and was involved in the remodelling of both it, *c.*1668-74 and Leslie House, 1667-74. He became Surveyor of the King's Works in Scotland in 1671 and was responsible for the rebuilding of Holyrood House in 1671-9. He bought Kinross estate in *c.*1681 and built the present mansion, 1685-90, a symmetrical design on the grand scale about an axial line focused on Loch Leven Castle. Bruce's work extended beyond Tayside to Lothian and Border areas including the remodelling of Thirlestane Castle (1670-6) and the design of Hopetoun House (1699-1703).

James Lorimer, 1818-90, Professor of Public Law, Edinburgh University, had 6 children. The third, John, born 1856 became a painter of distinction; the sixth, Robert, born 1864, grew up to be the renowned architect, knighted 1911, died 1929. Robert was apprenticed to Hew Wardrop, Edinburgh, and worked in London (George Bodley) and Edinburgh (James MacLaren and successors) before setting up his own practice in 1893. He is often compared with Sir Edwin Lutyens. Both were influenced by Arts & Crafts Movement, both were intuitive with sensuous appreciation of materials, both came from artistic families and were essentially countrymen. Having 'cut his teeth' on Kellie Castle (the family home) and Earlshall, Lorimer got a good grounding in his 1890s Colinton Cottages before entering the mansion house market with Rowallan (1903-6), Ardkinglass (1900-8), Formakin (1912-14). His Baronial was not Bryce's – it was refined, with good stonework and crisp vernacular detailing. The same romantic strain could transfer into a classical mould, Hill of Tarvit, 1905-7, or to academic Gothic, Thistle Chapel, 1909-11. His architecture *'has the refreshing qualities of things made by men's hands, lovingly, with an old song in their hearts'.* (Christopher Hussey). Robert's second son, Hew, is the eminent Scottish sculptor.

Above right *Kellie Castle*. Below *Lundie Cottage, Arncroach*

Victorian 'improvements' (the blight of many fine buildings in Fife) and then, in 1878 it was delivered into the caring hands of the Lorimer family who nursed it into the national treasure it is today. Sheltered on the north and east by belts of trees and Kellie Law, it commands superb views across the Forth. Crowsteps, gables, dormers, corbels, towers, strings, gargoyles, turrets, chimneys – all compose a dramatic poem in stone.

The castle's development is a 'Tale of Three Towers'. The north tower, late 15th/early 16th century, was built on a 14th-century tower. The east tower, 1573, was built 15m east of the north tower and in the early 17th century a fifth storey was added. In 1603-6 (dormerheads, 1606) a large L-shaped block linked north and east towers and provided the south tower – an architectural masterstroke. The four-bay, three-storey, link-block houses, on first floor, the Great Hall and Withdrawing Room (windows enlarged c.1663), and on upper, dormered storey, the striking Vine (ceiling painted by De Witt) and Earl's Rooms all featuring fine plaster and panel work. The magnificent walled garden which complements the castle building was re-designed by the young Robert Lorimer, son of Professor James Lorimer, the prime mover in the restoration; Robert Lorimer was also responsible for the corner **Garden House**, wallhead **doocot** and some of the interior decoration – his first designwork.

ARNCROACH
Hamlet west of Kellie Castle. **Lundie Cottage**, Main Road, 19th century cottage enlarged by Sir Robert Lorimer for his blacksmith in 1903 – note

typical flared vertical slating and ogee roofs on new bays. **Butler's House**, corner of Blinkbonny Road, 1749, is traditional.

3Gibliston, c.1820, was bought by Sir Robert Lorimer in 1916 for his own occupation. He provided some plain additions. A correct classical composition – masonry is rock-faced on basement, channelled on ground, and polished on first floors. Door and blind-balustraded windows are set in recessed arched panels.

ST MONANS (Colour pages C7 & C8)
Boats have fished out of St Monans since the 14th century and even in 1900 there were over 100 sail boats using the tidal harbour. Now fishing barely exists. The sole (major) employer is J N Miller & Sons who have been building small boats for over 200 years, using the harbour basins to fit them out. The form of the **Harbour** is not unlike that of Pittenweem – the original pier, 1596, becoming the central pier flanked on the east, 1865, and west, 1902, by piers and breakwaters, to create two basins.

At St Monans, during the 19th century, salt was still being extracted from the sea and coal from several outcrops near the shore (both occupations recalled by 18th-century Windmill Tower on Coal Farm which was used to pump seawater to salt pans).

Parish Church, Braehead, 14th century
Across the Clapper Bridge (two monolithic slabs over the Inweary Burn), on a cliff above the sea, stands this architectural masterpiece. The squat

St Monans Parish Church

Top *Interior of Kirk by R W Billings.*
Above *Elevation*

proportions of its spire and tower makes its silhouette one of the easily recognised Scottish kirks. It was built by David II in 1362-70, Sir William Dishington, Master of Works, in simple T-plan of chancel and transepts (intended nave never built). The crossing supports the tower, and low stone spire, faceted with tiny lucarnes, rises within the parapet. Ruinous, in 1772 it received *'partial reparation'* to be followed by William Burn's major restoration in 1826-8. External titivations – window tracery reformed, angle buttresses gabletted, chancel buttresses capped and its internal proportions radically altered by lowering floor level by 1m. Unusual external features include set-back gables (forming narrow parapet walks) and cornice enriched by small carvings of heads and 'buckle' corbels (i.e. they cast shadows which resemble human profiles). The vaulting detail is unusual and the bosses are of symbolic significance. Adding interest to the stark interior are customary credence-niche, 14th century and triple sedilia (on south wall of chancel) and double aumbry (on north wall). Suspended high in south crossing arch, is an 18th-century votive ship.

Station Road
Plunging down to the harbour it presents a story of the town's late 20th-century revival. To the east, along Hope Place, the **Town Hall** (former school), 1866, Thomas Currie, provides a gabled counterpoint to the nearby **Primary School,** 1987, by Regional Architect. The school assembles vernacular details; e.g. segmented-headed, steading-style windows, and loft hoists on gables and exploits slate skirtings on pantiled roofs.

To the west, **No 5 Inverie Terrace,** *c.*1840, black whinstone, while refurbished **Seaview,** late 19th century, keeps its decorative rainwater trappings. Lower-level **East Street** leads to modern housing, 1970, with vernacular inclinations, by Baxter Clark & Paul; also up slope at **Braid Court,** 1974. **2 West Street,** 17th century, retains its scrolled skewputt; whereas the **Maltings, Nos 15-17,** rehabilitated as flats in 1984, Cunningham Jack Fisher & Purdom, still display its characteristic ventilators. **1-9 Station Road,** 19th century, were carefully modernised in 1971. The huddle of the early fishing village can be experienced up **The Cribbs.** Note particularly the corbelled forestair and angle at **No 5,** 17th/18th century.

The picturesque façade of **West Shore** follows the line of the harbour wall. It contains what [87] were the most prestigious dwellings. **Nos 1,2,3** and **4** form typical 18th-century terrace, crisply painted with forestairs at **2** and **4** (pillar [88] supported); **5-7**, 18th century, rebuilt c.1830, has finialed stair fore-jamb. Pend extends invitation to back court and vaulted cellars. **21-25** all date from 18th century although roofs of **24** and **25** were raised in the late 19th century.

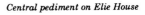

Above *Braid Court, St Monans.* left *Perspective view of Newark Castle by R S Lorimer showing proposed restoration and additions*

[89] **Newark Castle**, pre-16th century
Bought in 1649 by General Sir David Leslie, it is now a fragmented ruin, once subject of abortive restoration schemes by Sir Robert Lorimer, for Sir William Burrell in 1898-9.

[90] **Elie House**
Since 1697, every succeeding century has made another insensitive addition to this structure. The original, plain, three-storey five-bay south-facing house (which incorporated an earlier building) acquired c.1740 an uninspired west-facing addition. A stylish Ionic Venetian window at its south end and the carving in the pediment have been attributed to William Adam who is known to have carried out some work on the property but his design for a new house (illustrated in *Vitruvius Scoticus* c.1740) was never built. By the 19th century, the main entrance had been switched to the east front and marked by a balustraded baroque porch. A tower with octagonal lantern and ogee roof was wedged in the re-entrant (1854-5). When used as a convent in the 20th century an 'economy' chapel was added, 1958, Peter Whiston.

ELIE
Named from 'Ailie of Ardross', the island on

Central pediment on Elie House

Lady's Tower, Elie Ness, summerhouse for Lady Janet Anstruther of Elie House (described by Carlyle as *'a coquette and a beauty'*) who, when seabathing, used the rocky vaulted chamber at sea level as a changing room. On these occasions a bellman walked the streets of Elie and warned the natives to keep away. It was her wish to improve her own amenity that resulted in the razing of the nearby village of Balclevie and brought a curse on the House of Elie – an action which inspired Sir Walter Scott to introduce a similar incident in *Guy Mannering*.

which the Granary is built and from which the harbour evolved in 1582. The town, which became a Burgh of Barony in 1589, now incorporates Liberty and Williamsburgh and continues west directly into Earlsferry with which it was united in 1929. Today it is primarily residential, a place for retiral and a small holiday resort.

Parish Church, High Street (*above*)
The Georgian reconstruction of 1831 all but obliterates the original T-plan church of 1639. Its main feature, although somewhat aloof, is the clocktower centred on the south elevation, commissioned in 1726 by Sir John Anstruther.

Queen's Hotel and High Street, Elie

In the kirkyard flowers the Renaissance **mural monument** of Gillespie of the Muckle Yett.

High Street properties are generally 19th century. **Nos 55-57,** late 19th century, have key-blocked entrance and a characteristic feature much repeated in the town – an oriel window; **41-43,** c.1890, start in restrained manner on ground floor, blossom into semi-domed bows on first floor and develop into a riot of pediments (broken and segmental) on the second floor. On the corner of Chapman Place, **Queen's Hotel**, late-19th century (now flatted) idiosyncratic Victorian, comes complete with arcaded angle octagon.

Kingscroft, 18 High Street, 1862, John Currie, bears all the hallmarks of this local architect – black whinstone, stugged dressings, gabled entrance bay, round-headed doorways. **No 12, Rosemay**, 1895, is a spectacular venture into Victorian-Gothic. Note slim cast-iron mullions.

Towards the harbour **The Toft** Nos 1-5, 18th century, with piended masonry dormers, c.1860, make a brave terrace. In contrast the later, flanking dormers at **Seafield Bank**, The Toft, detract from the dramatic wallhead gable.

Rosemay – 12 High Street, Elie:- sombre, irregular, whinstone

Park Place, Elie

Park Place runs north from the Parish Church corner. On the east side are detached 19th century houses – **No 8** piended dormerheads and ubiquitous oriel; **10, Baldinnie**, early 19th century elegance; **Dunreggan**, c.1890, Scottish Baronial in full bloom (now subdivided). There are smaller houses on west side: **Nos 5-7**, Victorian terrace with steep-pitched gables; **19,** elaborate canted bay developed from broached angle; **33-37**, late Georgian terrace, and **39,** picturesque Victorian with tie-beam over Venetian window. To the west, **Nos 1-3 Bank**

Doorway from Muckle Yett, Gillespie House, Elie

Street, early 19th century, with interesting Doric pilastered shop front; **5,** late 19th century, still retains balustered glass lights above transom. **Royal Bank of Scotland,** Bank Street, early 19th century, has uneasy Baronial addition, 1864, David McGibbon. **Golf Hotel,** 1899, encapsulates the Scots Baronial style.

The ghost of Alexander Gillespie's Muckle Yett, 1682, demolished 1865 to facilitate road-widening, still haunts **South Street.** At **No 19, Southgate,** *c.*1860 (later modernised), a much-weathered doorway which survived the demolition still stands complete with console pilasters and key-blocked lintel. And at **Gillespie House,** No 25 (rebuilt 1870), John Currie, for his own occupation, the memorable Renaissance entrance of Muckle Yett has been incorporated. The magnificent baroque pediment is crowned with concave sundial dated 1682.

The **Castle,** South Street, 17th century, L-plan and back stair tower, dates probably from late 16th century. The finest traditional architecture in town, having all the right proportions, massing and ingredients. Inside are original painted ceilings and panelling.

At east end of South Street is a group of 17th century dwellings. **No 4, Seafort,** has massive chimney in back jamb; **Seven Gables** and **Easter Gables** (with 19th-century porch) are traditionally harled and crowstepped.

The **Terrace,** to the east, bristles with character; **No 8, Duddingston House,** late 17th century (additional storey, 18th century), is an impressive tenement; **7,** 18th century, enjoys

South Street, Elie

Top left *St Andrews Castle*. Top
right *'Haec Dies quam fecit
Dominus', Collegiate Chapel of St
Salvator*. Middle *Hradetzky Organ,
St Salvator's Chapel*. Left
*Reflections of Old St Andrews, South
Street*. Above *Sunday Ritual – 'The
Pier Walk'*

C 5

Top *Royal & Ancient Golf Club.*
Middle left *West Pitkierie Doocot.*
Middle right *Anstruther harbour.*
Above *Crail Chimney Pots.* Right '*A Fringe of Gold*'

C 6

Above '*A Fife Port*'. Left '*Pittenweem*'. Middle '*Masts and Houses, Pittenweem*'. Bottom '*St Monans*'

C 7

C 8

a pleasing symmetry (oriel-modern); **6, The Garden House**, *c*.1760, features Gibbs doorway; **1, Archibald House** (formerly Wade House as occupied for a time, by General George Wade), 1756 (much altered, 19th century), is topped off by a row of swept dormerheads. On the way to Earlsferry, **Marionville**, Links Place, *c*.1820, one out of many bigger, detached properties which line the route – bright sandstone, painted facings, neat dormers. At Liberty, there is the excellent **Fernbank**, 18th/early 19th century, architraved and corniced.

EARLSFERRY

It is said that the ancient ferry which plied between this point and North Berwick got its title from Macduff, Earl of Fife, as it made possible his escape from the clutches of Macbeth. The High Street, with no numbers, only names, achieves more regularity as it unfolds westwards.

Town Hall, 1864-72, John Currie
Mini-Baronial with slim-spired tower survivor of former Town House. It receives 19th-century support from **Waverley**, **Winston Cottage**, and **Viewforth**. Opposite are 18th-century houses, e.g. **The Rigging** and **Two Ways** (which owes much to its irregular fenestration).

The Gable, late-Georgian, sports a Venetian window and a Victorian extension; while the 20th-century reconstructed **Strathneuk** makes a significant contribution to the view east along High Street. **Turret Lodge**, 19th century, is a neat composition in Gothic, symmetric with one-window wings. Resting on the beach is **Sandford Cottage**, early 19th century, a doll-like dwelling with lattice windows.

Top *Earlsferry Town Hall, High Street*. Above *High Street*

Davaar (*above*), J Jerdan & Son, **Grange Neuk**, John McIntyre

Opposite:
Top *Pittenweem Harbour*. Middle left *St Monans Harbour, frontage*. Middle right *St Monans Harbour*. Bottom left *West Shore, Pittenweem*. Bottom right *North Fife landscape*

Kilconquhar Parish Church

Kinneuchar Inn

Kilconquhar with John Knox House in foreground

Two early 20th-century houses on **Grange Road** (north side of golf course), reflect the high-roofed, small-paned English-influenced Arts & Crafts.

On the hill behind, **Grange House** ranks as perhaps the most interesting building in the district. An early 18th-century laird's house in classical style with quadrant walls linking single-storey pavilions, at right angles to the main block. Quadrant walls advance to main gate piers and so complete the south forecourt. Although the house (destroyed in fire in 1860) is now a shell and one of the pavilions has been ponderously enlarged into a cottage, it remains a memorable composition.

KILCONQUHAR
In many ways a model village where every home strives to contribute charm – some perhaps, a little too much.

Parish Church, Main Street, 1819-21, R & R Dickson
Surveys all from its knoll beside the loch. Although the purist may have reservations its 24m angle-pinnacled tower is unequestionably distinctive and dominating. The Gothic cruciform plan is all angle-buttressed.

Kinneuchar Inn, Main Street, 18th century
Perpetuating the old name of the village, the centre block betrays its origins as a coaching inn. On **Main Street, No 25, Corner Croft**, 1752, and **No 31, Old Post House**, 18th century, retain many original features. A glimpse through the pend of **No 24, Knox House**, early 19th century, to its lochside garden confirms its idyllic situation. Fortunately the irregular fenestration at **No 26, Laigh Cottage**, 18th century, has been preserved.

This is an area of 'blue' whinstone (with cherry-cocking) and pale freestone dressings, e.g. **No 41, St Margaret's**, 1809; **26, Allan Cottage**, 19th century; and **Mayview**, 1788, with its interesting Gibbs entrance.

Kilconquhar Castle
A typical L-plan tower turreted on every external angle, encased within Kilconquhar House by William Burn, 1831, and David Bryce, 1839. Today after fire damage and radical pruning, it is the centrepiece of a Holiday Timeshare development.

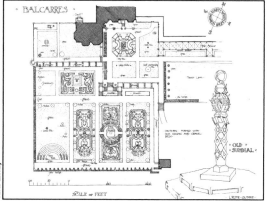

¹Balcarres, 1595 later extended
Balcarres lacks the magic of Kellie and Balcaskie. Although turrets, gables, dormers, massive bays and stacks proliferate this *embarras de richesse* is architecturally stodgy. The original L-plan tower house, 1595, of the Lindsays was submerged by massive additions – first, 1838-43, William Burn, and second, by eruptions of Scottish Baronial, mid-19th century, David Bryce. Internally the oak panelling, carving and plasterwork remain notable. The **gardens**, 19th century, with balustraded and buttressed terraces, and courts with fountains, possess a coherence lacking in the mansion; even the roofless **Chapel**, 1635, a strange mixture of classical and Gothic (compare ²Fordell Chapel), has more style. **North Lodge**, 1896-8, Sir Robert Lorimer, captures the spirit of 16th-century Scotland – harled walls, steep-pitched roofs, stone-sculptured dormers; **gate piers** capped by lions. Slightly less rugged but still displaying artistry in stone is Lorimer's **Estate Office**, 1903. Nearby, magnificent wrought-iron gates, c.1700, were imported from Cremona, Italy.

Top *Kilconquhar Castle by McGibbon & Ross*. Above *Balcarres Craig*. Left *Balcarres Gardens*

Colin, 3rd Earl of Balcarres (1652-1722) fought hard for the Stewarts and went into exile with them (1693-1700). On his return he developed, in 1705, **Colinsburgh** in order to resettle his 'demobbed' soldiers. He flirted again with 'The Cause' in 1715 but punishment on account of his age and friends at Court was light and he was merely confined to his home, Balcarres, for the rest of his life.

LARGOWARD

Once a mining village, its coal was sent to
Falkland Palace, c.1600. Now a quiet community
in an agricultural area extending over the
Riggin' o' Fife.

Parish Church, 1835, a former Chapel of Ease
– with birdcage belfry. **Durham Cottage**,
Durham Place, early 19th century, is a singular
Gothic composition of classical proportions.
Symmetry modified for its former role as a bank.

Gilston

393 **Gilston**, late 19th century
Large-scale two-storey 'box' of a mansion
enthusiastically detailed in classical style.
Symmetrical south front is framed by giant
angle-pilasters and pierced balustrade with urn-
finials. Taller, pedimented central bay contains
entrance (behind Ionic porch). East and west
fronts match. **Stable Building**, 1875, converted
to domestic use, is quadrangular with central
pend surmounted by sharp pointed spire.

COLINSBURGH

Virtually one street, Main Street, which, due to
the use of dark whinstone, has a gloomy aspect.
The **Town Hall**, Main Street, 1894-5 by A & A
C Dewar is plain with oversized porte-cochère
and strange entrance wings with flat-coned roofs.

Balgonar, 21 Main Street, early 19th century,
has typical dark whin rubble and freestone
dressings; **No 43, Corner House**, 18th century,
being earlier, has irregular fenestration. Up
North Wynd, Old Stable House, c.1840,
modernised with arches and hoist gables,

provides interest. **Fairfield Farmhouse**, 1717, retains moulded doorpiece; note sundial on skewputt. **Galloway Library**, Main Street, 1903, by Charles Davidson, strives to impress with barrel-vaulted entrance, rounded windowheads, balcony between corbelled roundels. In contrast is the quiet restraint of **No 46, The Cottage**, with Venetian window in central gablet. **No 79, Carvenom**, *c.*1840, is exceptional with carved hoodmoulds at all windows and consoled entrance canopy.

4 **Charleton House**, from 1749

A plain two-storey on raised basement, modified since by a procession of notable architects – some say William Adam and David Bryce, certainly William Burn, Sir Robert Lorimer, Reginald Fairlie – which, with intrusions by the owners, the Anstruthers, have deprived the mansion of a unity or even a consistent theme. Additional openings, *c.*1905, by Lorimer, in the richly pedimented south front, gave it a semi-Venetian appearance, which later suffered the indignity of a lean-to open porch. A rooflit salon and new single-storey north front, 1905-6, were designed by Lorimer. The Anstruthers in 1907 increased the front in height and embellished it with Roman busts. Internal plasterwork, decoration and chimneypieces are worthy of note.

5 **Newburn Old Church**

Said to have been built by monks from Dunfermline in 1166. A pre-Reformation shell in a placid rural setting. In the south-west corner of kirkyard lies Sir Robert Lorimer's family mural monument.

Top *Galloway Library, Colinsburgh – Municipal pomposity!* Above *Lorimer Family Grave – Newburn Kirkyard*

Coates House

6 **Coates House**, late 18th century
A later additional storey gives a Scottish

dimension to its classicism. Keystoned Victorian entrance is a refreshing change from the usual classical columns.

Strathairly House

397**Strathairly House**, mid/late 18th century
Refronted, *c*.1830, in classical manner, possibly by Robert Balfour. Additional bays provide symmetry but advanced pedimented centre is overwhelmed by Ionic porch. At the rear the original 18th-century round stairtower has been preserved.

UPPER LARGO (Kirkton of Largo)
Largo district, which enjoys the shelter of Largo Law, has been peopled since earliest times. The impressive **Standing Stones** at Lundin Links possibly date from the time of the Druids. At **Strathairly**, Bronze Age cists, *c*.1500 BC, have been discovered.

Upper Largo Parish Church

Parish Church, 17th century
Tower, 1628, and chancel, 1623, incorporated into cruciform church, 1816-17, by Alexander Leslie. The sharp pointed spire, obelisk finials and outsize crenellation give a spiky appearance to this elevated place of worship. The **kirkyard** walls, 1657, contain at sides of gate a small square, early 19th century offertory & gate house. The **Manse**, 1770, increased in height in 1837, presents a plain façade, save mini-bracketed window sills. Behind the church the **Church Place** houses climb the brae in neat, painted fashion. **Rose Cottage**, 3 North Feus. The three bowed dormers and robust triple end stacks attract attention.

Wood's Hospital

Wishart

Sir Andrew Wood, *c*.1455-1539. His legendary exploits in the *Yellow Carvel*, particularly in 1498 when he routed the English fleet in the Forth, earned him later the nickname *'Scottish Nelson'*. His successes were rewarded by James III who presented to him the Lands of Largo and by Charter, 1491, licensed the building of *'a tower or fortalice with iron gates'*. Today the only relic of his castle is an early 17th century tower with shallow cone roof. There is still evidence of the canal (approx 1/2 km long and claimed to be the first in Scotland) which he constructed from the castle to the church so that he could be transported to church in an eight-oared barge.

Wood's Hospital, Woodlaw Park, 1830, James Leslie
The vigorous Jacobean-style makes a magnificent south front. The central advanced gable sets the pace. It carries scrolled crockets on slabbed skews, a birdcage pinnacle and obelisk terminals. The octagonal form of the flues is repeated at the gate piers. The original Woods Hospital, *c*.1665, designed by Robert Mylne, King's Master Mason, provided for *'13 indigent and enfeebled persons'* and included *'services of gardener, porter and chaplain'*. Adjacent **Eden Cottage**, St Andrews Road, 1756, has simple dignity and displays a Gibbs surround at main entrance.

South Feus is a quiet byway of diverse, early 19th-century properties, which enjoy the open view south across the Forth.

98**Largo House**, 1750, John Adam
This desolate shell of a grand classical mansion stands in full view of the main road. Years of neglect have failed to destroy the fine proportions of the seven-bay symmetrical front, its three-bay pedimented centre, Ionic (dated) entrance, and broad steps. Evidence of 1831 wings still exists, also the square, walled 17th-century garden. **Eagle Gate**, late 18th century. Stylish vermiculated piers, key-pattern above and capped by eagles. **East Gate**, late 18th century, has swagged bands supporting fluted urn finials.

The umbrella, it is claimed, was invented by a Largo man hence its nickname *'Nether Lairgie'*. Alexander Selkirk had an umbrella and that is why it features in illustrations of Robinson Crusoe.

Alexander Selkirk, 1676-1721, *(above* in Stewart Burnett's fine statue of 1885) was Daniel Defoe's inspiration for Robinson Crusoe. The statue in the niche at 101 Main Street, Lower Largo, marks the site of the thatched cottage where Selkirk was born. The wilful son of a shoemaker, he ran off to sea where, after quarrelling with his captain he was put ashore on the deserted island of Juan Fernandez where he spent over four years.

Lundin Links Hotel

LOWER LARGO (Seatown of Largo)
Another one-street village at the bottom of a cliff where 18th-century weavers' and fishermen's dwellings jostled irregularly for space. By the 19th century there was a steamboat service from Newhaven. With the arrival of the railway in 1856, the village became fairly prosperous. This is reflected in the architecture. **Harbour** dates from *c*.1770, extended early 19th century.

Crusoe Hotel, *c*.1850 (former granary)
Three-storey piended south wing presents a sturdy quayside bastion to the Forth. The dormers, arches and gable forestair of north wing relate to the domestic scale of its surroundings. **Bridgend House** and its range of outbuildings, early 19th century, retain much of their original character.

Old Railway Viaduct, 1856-7
Four enormous arches with expressed ashlar voussoirs master the valley of the Kiel Burn. In the shadows where once there was a flax-spinning mill stands **Seatoun Place**, 1984, not unpleasing version of the vernacular.

Cardy Networks, Main Street, a fascinating relic of a small 18th-century commercial enterprise. **Works Buildings,** 1867, three-parallel brick ranges form east boundary of walled garden (once bowling green for workers). At garden gate, **Cardy Cottage,** 1885, was originally twin villas for senior staff. **Cardy House,** 1871, the owner's house and typical product of Victorian affluence. Internal, ornamental plasterwork attributed to itinerant Italian craftsmen.

LUNDIN LINKS
Virtually a 19th-century suburb of Lower Largo. Lundin Links is now mostly holiday and dormitory accommodation.

Lundin Links Hotel *(left)*,
1900, Peter L Henderson
An architectural curiosity divorced from any local tradition – red brick and tiles, black and white half-timber insets, jerkin-headed gables. **Crescent Road** was the address of the affluent Victorians. **No 25, Bourtree Brae House**, 1859, is much gabled and much chimneyed. **No 15, Old Calabar,** and **No 21, Oldfield**, whin and freestone with decorative eaves and barges; both *c*.1865 by James Campbell Walker.

99Lundin Tower
Relic of Old Lundin House demolished 1876, with late-18th century parapet and turreted south angles. **Lundin Doocot,** converted 19th century, was originally 18th-century laundry, hence the unusual Gothic-styled windows.

00Pitcruivie Castle, late 15th century Romantic site overlooking bridge over Keil Burn softens forbidding aspect of the ruinous rectangular tower (with suggestion of small stair jamb at north-west angle).

On a site near Morton Farm, Tentsmuir, a Stone Age site was discovered in 1957. There was evidence in the layering of refuse in middens and a large collection of stone implements of seasonal camping for a period of over 700 years, some 8000 years ago. Just to the north of the site is the **Morton Lochs Nature Reserve** where at migration time, wild fowl and waders are worth seeing. To the east, along the coastal strip, is Tentsmuir Nature Reserve where the wild fowl roost and seals assemble on the sand banks.

North Fife
The area lies north of the Eden Valley and includes the valley of the Motray Water and communities bordering the Tay. Towns are small and much of the land is devoted to agriculture. To the east, the Tentsmuir forest covers the coastal plain.

01Craigie House, c.1850, off B945
A central curvilinear gable makes the main impact. The stepped and shouldered gables and **02**gablets are merely echoes. **St Fillan's Church,** c.1500, *The Parish Church of St Philans, or Forgen, that was one of the Kirks of Priory of St Andrews.* Rectangular shell with north aisle, c.1600. The bold interconnecting arch has moulded imposts. Interesting stones, 17th **3**century, in **kirkyard. Vicarsford Cemetery Chapel,** 1895-7, T M Cappon. A very French Gothic concoction standing tall on hillock – distinctive copper-green roof with flèche.

Above *Vicarsford Cemetery Chapel.*
Left *Gate Piers at Scotscraig*

4Scotscraig
This estate on the heights above Tayport commands excellent views over St Andrews Bay.

In the old Parish Kirkyard, Tayport, many of the inscriptions refer to shipmasters who, under sail, enjoyed the thriving continental trade.

Reputedly named after Sir Michael Scott of Balwearie to whom it was feued in the reign of Alexander I, the Sharp family held it (1667-80) during the time the Archbishop was slain on Magus Moor in 1679. **Gate piers**, 1620, Renaissance with globular finials, stand forlorn in field dyke, west of Scotscraig Mains. **Archway**, 1667, also Renaissance, marks entrance to walled gardens. The Archbishop's arms and initials are on the keystone.

TAYPORT
Once appropriately called Ferryport-on-Craig it began as a few ferrymen's dwellings. During James II's reign strategic importance prompted the building of a castle (not unlike Claypotts) which now exists only in names, such as Castle Street. The arrival of the railway, in 1842, and the rail ferry in 1846, precipitated industrial growth (sawmill 1850, spinning works 1864, cloth mill 1865, engineering works 1875) and the construction of the Tay Rail Bridge, opened 1878, consolidated its links with Dundee.

Two views of former Parish Church, Tayport showing the leaning tower

Former Parish Church, part 1794 Converted to, **Community Centre**, 1988, it is mainly 1825. The most interesting feature is a corbelled tower with pyramid roof. The appreciable 'lean' is almost certainly due to lack of support from the Scotscraig Vault below. Around junctions of **Tay Street**, **Whitenhill**

and **School Wynd** some early 19th century vernacular buildings survive (with modernisation), e.g. **Nos 1-3** (pity about glass bricks), **20-24 Whitenhill, 2** and **4 Butter Wynd, 90-92 Tay Street. No 4 School Wynd,** late 18th century, has walled forecourt, note decorative lintels at **Nos 15** and **20 Rose Street** and the skewputts and margins at **No 8 Greenside Place**, late 18th century.

Harbour. Rebuilt in 1847 by Thomas Grainger, so that paddle-steamers plying across the Firth of Tay to Broughty Ferry could accommodate (on rails) loaded goods trucks; abandoned when the Tay Rail Bridge opened in 1878. Nearby **11 Inn Street** (former Old Scotscraig Inn), *c.*1800, presents regular front to Tay; behind is large stone-vaulted icehouse (now garage). **Nos 17-21 Inn Street** have pleasantly irregular frontage dating from the 18th century, and feature lugged lintels. Tayport's nautical architecture includes **Pile Lighthouse**, *c.*1848, offshore stilted box structure with conical roof and landbound **East** and **West Lighthouses**, West Common, 1823, Robert Stevenson. East Lighthouse retains railed balcony and graceful domed cupola.

Our Lady Star of the Sea R C Church, Queen Street, 1938-9, Reginald Fairlie Pleasing proportions emphasised by white-rendered smooth finish. The square entrance porch is deftly broached into octagonal tower and marked by Hew Lorimer's sculpture, *Our*

Top *Detail of tower, Tayport Parish Church.* Centre *Infill housing in Tayport by District Council.* Left *Our Lady Star of the Sea RC Church* Above *Ave Stella Maris by Dr Hew Lorimer on tower.*

Lady; the Regency cottage at **No 2 William Street**, 1810, has broad-eaved roof which oversails the bowed projections flanking the entrance. **No 36**, *c.*1830, acquired single-storey wings, *c.*1850, and heavy formal perron, *c.*1930, to serve its Doric entrance. **Nos 7-21 Isla Place**, Albert Street, late 19th century, Victorian terrace built to house Tay Bridge workers.

The Tay Road Bridge – north to Dundee (The Tay Bridge is visible at extreme left)

Tay Road Bridge, 1963-6, Fairhurst & Partners
A simple concrete multi-span supporting 2km long incline which exaggerates the perspective effect viewed from the Fife landfall.

NEWPORT-on-TAY
Almost exclusively Victorian. Created for Dundee 'jute barons' so that, from a smoke-free environment, they could watch the reek of their factory chimneys across the Tay.

Parish Church, Blyth Street, 1869-70, Alexander Johnston
Upward thrust of north tower breaks free from preponderant roof. **St Mary's Episcopal Church**, High Street, 1886-7, T M Cappon, more restrained than his Vicarsford, even the north-east porch subdued by jerkin-headed roof.

At the bottom of **High Street, Trinity United Free Church**, 1881, C & L Ower, is appropriately exuberant High Victorian from spirelet and crested ridges to pyramid-capped gatepiers. Nearby, **Newport Hotel, Boat**

The story of the Tay Crossings could fill more than one volume. First, from the 15th century, there were the huddles on the small ferry boats tacking from Tayport and Woodhaven. When Dr Johnson crossed to Dundee in 1773 he characteristically complained *'though the water was not wide we paid four shillings'*. From 1875 there were the smart parades on the upper decks of the 'Fifies'. By the 1890s competition was provided by the comfortable, warm First Class carriages which shuttled back and forth across the rail bridge. Today there are the car commuter queues on the Road Bridge.

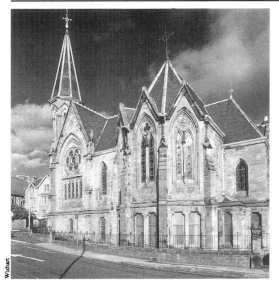

Road, 1806, is a former coaching inn with artisan classical details while **Nos 4-6 High Street**, early 19th century, is a quaint classical composition (former estate office for Tayfield).

Left *Tayfield*. Top left *Trinity UF Church*. Top right *Parish Church*. Above *4-6 High Street – toytown classic*

Tayfield, 1788, Robert Anderson Enlarged and dressed in Tudor style, 1829-30, by George Smith. Its owner, the Berry family, is synonymous with Newport and the estate overlooks the Terminal of the ferry which the Berrys were instrumental in founding. **North Lodge**, High Road, 1821, J Gillespie Graham, is broad-eaved and lattice-windowed.

Ferry Terminal, Boat Brae, is now not in use. Two large semicircular barrel vaults, late 19th century, signal Telford's 1823 ramped pier. Italianate west wing, *c.*1880, C & L Ower, heavily capitalled but with some whimsical touches. East along Tay Street, **Nos 8-10,** *c.*1840, well-detailed classical with V-plan bays, **No 56, Canisbay Lodge,** *c.*1860, in Tudor dress with timber porch to match; **No 58, Ravenscraig,** *c.*1840, is a former coaching inn, in austere Georgian; **Nos 60-64,** *c.*1840, in prevalent Italianate style – low-pitched, broad-eaved, finely detailed.

Guide plates and milestones, such as the 1824 cast-iron one (*above*) are a feature of Fife. The Kingdom has been particularly fortunate not only in possessing well-designed cast-iron guide plates and milestones but also having people who are prepared to preserve them. In *c.*1810, the Outh and Nivingston Trust adopted a surprisingly modern-styled design of milestone for their road from Dunfermline to Rumbling Bridge. In north-east Fife along the Great Fife Road from Pettycur to Newport cast-iron plates produced by Alexander Russell, Kirkcaldy Foundry, dated 1824, mark the miles and at the same time record history — the old ferries at Pettycur and Newport, the old staging posts, such as New Inn.

Top 10-12 Boat Brae. Right Drinking fountain

Andrew Heiton Junior, 1823-94, architect, is best known for his French château-style Atholl Palace Hotel, Pitlochry.

Drinking Fountain, 1882
Embodying the spirit of the Victorian age – look what we can do in iron! West are two mansions: **St Serf's,** High Road, 1865-6, Andrew Heiton jun, now Eventide Home, and **Balmore,** West Road, *c.*1860, both Italianate style complete with towers.

Abercraig, 2 West Road, 1840
Dower house for Tayfield, built on the cliff edge.
To the road, a single-storey with semicircular
Doric porch; facing the river, down cliff face, it is
three storeys with canted bay.

Nos 28-58 West Road presents an
extraordinary sequence of early 19th-century
architecture: **Nos 28-36**, The Terrace, c.1840, of
one-up and one-downs, behind intricate Tudor
façade; **Nos 44-46**, Broadheugh, 1828, Italianate
mini-villa; **Nos 48** and **50**, twin Jacobean, **No
52**, Castle Cottage, 1812, Strawberry Hill
Gothic; and **Nos 54-58**, Heathfield, early 19th
century twins, (ignore timber extension.) **Nos
53-59 West Road**, The Castle, early 19th
century, continues the same folly-like character,
with tubular toy-fort towers. Victorian Newport
hides its product of the 1930s up William Street:
Rio Community Centre, former cinema, with
monstrous appliqué concrete modelling.

Woodhaven, an old ferry terminal.
Woodhaven Farmhouse, 92 Riverside Road,
c.1820, is a former inn, smartly painted pink
and cream. **Mars Cottage**, 97 Riverside Road,
c.1800, has 'lying' panes dating from the 1830s.
On the road to the pier the **Joiner's Workshop**,
1799, well-built, utilitarian.

WORMIT
Wormit was a hamlet until Tay Rail Bridge
opened in 1878. Then it became, like Newport, a
dormitory for Dundee.

Tay Rail Bridge, 1882-7, W H Barlow & Sons
Lacks the dramatic profile of its Forth
counterpart but the sheer length (3.5km) of this
fragile link with its graceful sweep into the
opposite coastline commands admiration. The
stumps of its short-lived predecessor, 1871-8,
Thomas Bouch, collapsed 1879, can still be seen
18 m downstream.

Wormit Shop, 1895, corner of Mount Stewart
Road, is an extravaganza in black and white.
Above the canted window are gablets, dormers
and turret with elongated ogee roof. **23
Naughton Road**, c.1880, is a kind of Roman
villa with iron-columned five-arched loggia.

Top *Rio Community Centre*. Above
Wormit shop

Wormit claims it was the first village
in Scotland to have electricity. The
builder of most of its early houses,
Alexander Stewart, had a windmill
on Wormit Hill which was
supplemented by a steam (later coal
gas) generator. In 1930 the
connection to the main grid took place.

Valley of Motray Water has been for centuries
the route followed by travellers heading north to
ferry or, today, Road Bridge.

405Sandford Hill Hotel, 1913, M H Baillie-Scott
English Arts & Crafts style enthusiastically
meets the challenge of an old quarry site – steep,
406sweeping roofs and pergolas. **Cruivie Castle**,
late 15th/early 16th century, near South
Straiton Farm, is a gaunt L-shaped ruin with
main entrance, unusually, in main block and not
re-entrant.

KILMANY

A quiet village with grassy banks and hawthorn
trees.

Above *A sympathetic sweep of Arts
and Crafts at Sandford Hill Hotel.*
Right *Kilmany Parish Church*

In the steading at Rathillet
House can be identified a two-storey
dwelling which allegedly was
occupied by David Hackstoun, one of
the party who assassinated
Archbishop Sharp in 1679.

Parish Church, 1768
Endearing simplicity of round-headed windows
and tall belfry. Pulpit and sounding board are
original.

Kilmany House, 1914-19, Reginald Fairlie
In South African-Dutch style with curvilinear
gables, pantiles and shutters. Later feature,
1927, is octagonal dining room with faceted roof;
now subdivided.

Dr Thomas Chalmers, 1780-1847.
The sixth child in a family of
fourteen of Baillie John Chalmers
was born at 35 High Street,
Anstruther Easter. He was one of
the outstanding Scottish church
leaders of the 19th century. A prime
mover in the Disruption of 1843 he
became the first Moderator of the
Assembly of the Free Church of
Scotland. From 1803 to 1815 he was
minister at Kilmany where his
evangelical preaching drew crowds
to his services. It is said he practised
his sermons on the rocky shores of
his native town.

407Rathillet House, *c*.1790
Fashionable two-storey symmetry and flat arch
voussoirs over central doorway.

408Mountquhanie, *c*.1820, J Gillespie Graham
An impressive classical façade. The fluted
parapet conceals the roof and emphasises
rectangularity of the frontage. The six-bayed
main block manages to centre on a Doric portico,
and both supporting wings have pedimented
centre bays. All sit on substantial basement.
Behind, only a crumbled tower remains of 16th-
century **Mountquhanie Castle** (*see next page*).

According to the legend *Earl Beardie* (Alexander, 4th Earl of Crawford, d.1453) can be seen at the stroke of twelve on the last night of the year playing cards with the devil in his old seat, Lordscairnie Castle.

Mountquhanie

Lordscairnie Castle,
late 15th/early 16th century
Once an impressive four-storey tower house with staircase jamb on north-west. Now like a block of nibbled cheese in a marshy field.

MOONZIE
An upland rural parish at the source of the Moonzie Burn, tributary of the Motray Water.

Moonzie Parish Church

Parish Church, *c.*1625
Occupies the elevated site of medieval church, east gable specifically whitewashed to serve as a landmark for ships in St Andrews Bay – hence its nickname *the visible kirk*. Square-columned belfry on west and ball finial on east gable are its only embellishments. **Moonzie House** (former manse), 1804, extended to T-plan by front jamb, 1848, William Ramsay and John Brunton. Extensive 'offices', 1806, confirm the relative opulence of 19th-century rural ministers.

Near **Luthrie, Colluthie House,** 18th century (back), Baronial (front), 1883, James McLaren & Son. **Carphin House,** Luthrie, late

18th/early 19th-century. Plain block given 19th century pedimented porch and dormers, and attractively rendered in pale pink. **Lodge,** c.1900, Sir Robert Lorimer, in utilitarian mood.

[413] **Creich Parish Church,**
1829-32, William Stirling
Diagonal buttresses at all corners; at tower they rise to pinnacles linked by arcaded parapets. Confusingly Creich Castle and Old Creich Kirk (St Devenic Parish Church) stand further up hill beyond Brunton.

[414] **Collairnie Tower** (south of A913),
16th century
As at Balcomie, a fine architectural feature has become an embarrassment as the work of the farm circumscribes the surviving five-storey tower dated 1581 (with turnpike jamb). Angle turrets have been sliced by later oversailing roof but arms and other carved details above the entrance door remain. Tempera-painted ceilings barely survive.

On the ridge north of Motray Water sits **Gauldry,** originally rural and weaving centre; now modern schemes cater for its mainly dormitory role. Of the older buildings there are **Balgove Farmhouse,** early 19th century (former tollhouse, inn and staging station) – picturesque group, crisply painted white with black margins. **Woodend House,** late 18th century, at edge of Dandies Wood, has Doric-columned doorway and neat L-plan outbuildings.

Top *Collairnie Tower.* Above *Balmerino in 1837*

Naughton Castle, 16th century (now ruinous), was a stronghold of the Hay family (a panel dated 1625 records work carried out by Peter Hay). It is said that a lamp burned on top of its tower to guide shipping in the Firth of Tay.

[415] **Naughton House,** 1793
Unusual dog-legged stair leads to a Doric entrance in the central balustraded bow. Later alterations in 1890 and in c.1900 provided an ogee-roofed tower in the east wing, and in re-entrant angle, a circular service stair corbelled to square. In the hall is an excellent Adam-style ceiling and spectacular curved cantilevered stairway. Although little remains of **Naughton Castle,** 16th century, the ancillary buildings are of interest: **summerhouse,** early 19th century, contains 15th-century tracery, possibly from Balmerino Abbey; a fine lectern-style **doocot,** dated 1750; **game larder,** c.1880, unconventional two-storey; Gothic **laundry block,** c.1832; **Gate Lodge,** c.1832, with semi-octagonal porch.

Wishart

BALMERINO
Small hamlet beside Abbey, servicing 18th-century harbour trade and 19th-century fishing. Physicians advised James V's first wife, *'go to Balmerino for that has the best airs of any place in the Kingdom'*. To the east, the **Parish Church**, 1811, plain Georgian is softened by Gothic treatment in 1883-4 by C & L Ower.

Balmerino Abbey
Cistercian Monastery founded by Alexander II and his mother Ermengarde in 1226, but burning by English in 1547 and pillaging by Reformers of 1559 and others have left few significant remnants. The outline of the nave and transepts of 13th-century church is just decipherable. The adjacent cloister (unusually in north-west quadrant) lies in the garden of the farmhouse. Beside the north transept springs a barrel-vaulted Sacristy, with newel stair, and next (the finest part extant), the Chapter House, rebuilt in the 15th century with vault supported by octagonal shafted piers with enriched capitals. A narrow barrel-vaulted parlour and two cells (all 13th century) complete the ruined range. Of the detached Abbot's house, probably 15th century, only two vaulted cellars survive.

Balmerino Farm Steading contains fragments from Abbey but its **Barn**, 15th century, retains distinctive steep-pitched west gable (doocot

Wishart

Balmerino Abbey as seen by Defoe: *'nothing worth observation, the very ruins being almost eaten up by time.'*

Above *Barn doorway at Balmerino Farm Steading.* Above right *Displaced portico makes a grand entrance at David Scrymgeour-Wedderburn Memorial Square*

boxes on inner face) and original pointed arch doorway (formed with two stones). To the south, in memory of scion of Wedderburns killed at Anzio is **David Scrymgeour-Wedderburn Memorial Square**, 1948, by H J Scrymgeour-Wedderburn. Traditional pantiled cottages, given a classical formality, emphasised by Doric-columned portico and pediment (improvised from Birkhill, family home).

Old Inn (former coaching inn), 18th century, masses with **Bridgend**, early 19th century, formed out of two salmon fishers' bothies. Across the road, another two storey and cottage pairing – **Bridgend House** and **Commalon**, 18th century.

CREICH
Amidst the quiet uplands two scraps of history: **St Devenic's Church**, late 14th century; a typical narrow roofless rectangle with central south chapel, *c*.1538. A savage 1621 reconstruction left only one original window – 417the lancet at east end of north wall. **Creich Castle,** 16th century, a ruined tower house, moth-eaten with age, had associations with Cardinal Beaton and Mary Bethune. There are indications of corbelled angle turrets and elaborate cornice at parapet level. Nearby, remains of small circular **gate tower** (now harled with lean-to roof) and lectern **Doocot**, 1723.

Creich Castle

BRUNTON
Picturesque, unfrequented upland village near source of Motray Water. Once a centre of cottage-weaving.

Manse of Creich, 1815-16, Just & Carver Typical classical symmetry. Behind, the **Druid**

Circle, two concentric rings discovered south west of manse in 1816, resited 1817. **The Beeches**, 1847, with three piended dormers nestles, neat and compact. At its gable the road leads to the 19th-century **Croft** and **Cherry Bank** which retain much original charm. **Free Church School**, School Row, 1846 has a *burning bush* motif, while **Burnside**, 19th century, still has byre wing with pigeon-holed gable at right angles to original cottage. **Dendale Farmhouse**, early 19th century, carefully modernised; detached building opposite, probably early 19th-century weaving shed.

Birkhill

¹⁸Birkhill, 1780
Plain core built beside the River Tay with 1812-14 wings overwhelmed by Tudor Baronial treatment in 1857-9, David Bryce. His balustraded circular entrance tower, with dome-headed caphouse, is pivotal to the composition.

RIAS Library/Miller

McKean/McG & R

McKean/McG & R

Two views by McGibbon & Ross of Ballinbreich Castle

¹⁹Ballinbreich Castle, 14th century
Pronounced Balmbreich. In 1312 the Leslies acquired the lands of Barony of 'Balnebrich' on the south shore of the Tay. The original building was extended in the 16th century and largely reconstructed late 16th century (c.1572 has been suggested). The somewhat inaccessible ruins remain awe-inspiring. L-shaped range (west and south) and L-shaped curtain wall (east and north) enclose a rectangular courtyard. The vaulted ground floor of the west range contains the kitchen with massive projecting chimney breast. In the south range the original gateway

Lindores Abbey was founded in 1178, by David, Earl of Huntingdon ('Sir Kenneth' of Sir Walter Scott's *Talisman*), brother of William the Lion. It was not to become just a sleepy Benedictine house of prayer or, by Royal appointment, supplier of apples and pears to Falkland Palace. Within its walls Alexander, only son of Alexander III, died; Edward I held court and extracted sworn allegiance from Scottish representatives; Sir William Wallace celebrated his victory at Black Earnside; John Balliol held court; Gilbert Hay of Errol vowed to defend Robert the Bruce to the death.

at east end has been enclosed by a later trance and the new entrance was defended by gun-looped round tower. At west end of this range, where original floor levels are now uncertain, there are traces of a chapel – three 14th-century sedilia, and a piscina and aumbry. In the re-entrant between the arms of the ranges, is a later, finely detailed staircase.

420**Parkhill Farm**, steading; south-east part, 18th century. Mill, rebuilt in the 19th century, with wheel and flume, making an attractive group in traditional pantile, whin and freestone.

421**Lindores Abbey**, founded 1178 (*above and left*) Here, the Benedictine Order enjoyed 400 years of rich living (the monks pioneered fruit growing in this area) but in 1559 John Knox commanded them to *cast away their monkish habits*. The remains are even less significant than those at Balmerino. The conventional layout of church, chapterhouse and cloister can just be identified on the ground but only the parlour, slype and round-arched south-west gateway are upright (to a limited extent). Across the road is the ruin of a 13th-century barn. The Abbey's red freestone, from Hyrnside, has been much plundered for the buildings in the district.

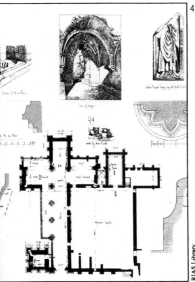

NEWBURGH
Early Newburgh was self-sufficient, a Royal Burgh by 1631. In the remote north-west corner of Fife, it could rely on the seasonal fruit harvest and salmon fishing. Above all, it thrived on weaving. All waned as industrialisation ruined the cottage weaving industry and absorbed most

Newburgh from the north in 1837

of the population into linoleum manufacture (in the late 19th century). When, in 1978, the Tayside Floorcloth Company closed, the Royal Burgh received a shock from which it is only now starting to recover.

Parish Church, Cupar Road, 1905-6, Thoms & Wilkie
Late Gothic composition in dark rubble with buff dressings. The crocketed pinnacle motif on the squat tower is repeated along the street front. In the classical competition between the two hotels, the late artisan doorway of **The Abbey**, 18th century (top storey, 19th century), is no match for the Doric doorway, frieze, cornice and quoins at **The George**, 1811.

To the speeding motorist the architecture of the **High Street** has a drab uniformity. Closer inspection reveals interesting variations.

Nos 32, 34, 36-40 have original 19th-century shopfronts and **No 32** has a good Victorian doorway with Venetian windows above. **No 42**, c.1830, has distinctive classical style including Doric detailing at recessed doorway; at **Nos 58-60**, unusual over-door panel of sailing ship dated 1752. Note sculptured details at **Nos 62, 64 and 68**, all early 19th century, especially quatrefoils on pilasters at **No 62**. The first-floor architraves at **Nos 35-39**, early 19th century, and two-way forestair at **No 27**, 18th century, quoined and key-blocked close and door openings at **Nos 41** and **49-51**, both early 19th century; all contribute to the street architecture.

32 High Street, Newburgh

Above *Town House, Newburgh.*
Below *High Street, Newburgh (No 81 on extreme left)*

Town House, 1808, John Speed

Simple civic dignity whose square tower, centred on classical frontage contains arched doorway with matching Venetian window above (the balustraded steps are Victorian). At the belfry stage the tower is broached to octagonal and crowned by crenellated parapet and spire – a monument to local craftsmen.

No 81 High Street, *c.*1800, is an exceptional building of classical formality with flyover steps serving Ionic-columned entrance. **Tolbooth Close**, 1981, L A Rolland & Partners. Incorporated Old Granary, *c.*1800, into attractive residential scheme. **Nos 83-93**, 1840, is another classical block. The bow-fronted dormers with 'lying' panes are original. **St Katherine's Close**, 1971, L A Rolland & Partners, blends pleasantly with its older neighbours. Three arches afford attractive glimpses of the Tay.

Lindores Lodge, 1815

A virtuoso display of masons' skills in curious artisan classical style including assortment of urns and relief sculptures. On the south side of the High Street are demonstrated the slight variations in architecture of 18th century and 19th century, e.g. the change in scale, particularly the windows, between **Nos 167-173** – 18th century (note thatch roof) and **Nos 175** and **177**, early 19th century; the Victorian dormerheads on **187** and the simplicity of **Nos 213** to **189**, early 19th century. On the north

side of the High Street the plain street frontage of **Nos 154-178**, all built *c*. 1800, contrasts with the embellishments on **Nos 186-8** and **190-2**, and Venetian at **Nos 194-6**, all late 18th century.

Tayview Hotel, *c*.1840
With its rusticated treatment makes a robust terminal to the street frontage; while **Tay Bridge Tavern**, Clinton Street, early 19th century, looks out from its elaborately pilastered shell, east along the High Street.

Barns o' Woodside, 18th century
Malt-barns, converted into house in 1898, enjoy magnificent views across the Tay. A romantic composition to suit steep site. Original brick-arched windows have been retained and carved stones from the Abbey have found their way into buttressed walls.

To the west of Newburgh, **Mugdrum** dates from the early 18th century (some parts even earlier). Before the 1745 Rising it was the home of Lord George Murray, Jacobite General. After reconstructions *c*.1790, and *c*.1840, the fenestration on the south elevation achieved some formality; although the advanced gabled wings on the north elevation, high above the Tay, are more exciting.

Mugdrum Cross (*above*) is one of two ancient stones which lie to the west and south of Newburgh. It stands on a small knoll in the grounds of Mugdrum. Its worn reliefs and Celtic patterns suggest an age of 1300 years. Woodriffe Road leads to **Macduff's Cross** – the focal point of hotly disputed legends. Sir Walter Scott judged the view from it as '*one of the finest and noblest in the world*'.

Pitcairlie – note the three recesses in the square tower which once contained beehives

Pitcairlie, late 16th century
A composite building where each addition

Denmylne Castle *(above)* was the residence of the antiquary Sir James Balfour, whose collection of manuscripts formed the basis of much of authenticated Scottish history.

sought no quarter from what went before. Of the original late 16th-century Z-plan only the four-storey tower (with parapets and rounds) survives, albeit like a withered limb, on the 18th-century main block. Originally this block *c.*1730, was to have been of seven bays with central Venetian entrance, but the two east bays were never built. After more additions in 1740 and 1815, the east gable of the 1730 block acquired a full height bow. After three years' gestation the bow produced a two-storey bay. Inside is a good semi-elliptical stairway, some fine panelling, *c.*1730, and wall paintings, 1833.

[423] **Denmylne Castle**, late 16th century
Even in its ruinous state this small, frugal block (originally a Royal mill given to the Balfours in 1509 by James IV) remains impressive. Three-storey with two apartments on each floor. The turnpike stair was in back jamb while small fore jamb contained either garderobe or private stair linking first to second floor.

Inchrye Lodge, 1827, R & R Dickson
Broad-eaved Gothic house, by Lindores Loch, based on octagonal plan.

Lindores House

[424] **Lindores House**, *c.*1820, perhaps James Mylne. Austere bow fronted pavilion, the consoled cornices to the windows and sills only embellishment. Restoration of the lying-pane glass on the lower windows would restore its style.

[25]**Abdie Parish Church**, 1827, William Burn
(succeeded James Mylne and W H Playfair)
Stands in rural isolation. A plain rectangle,
expressed in round-arched style, complements
tower belfry which displays unusual Italianate
tendencies.

Old Parish Church, Abdie

Old Parish Church, Abdie, (St Magridin's)
consecrated 1242 by David de Bernham, Bishop
of St Andrews. Originally a hallowed, narrow
rectangle, it acquired, in the 17th century, a
north transept (eventual burial place of Balfours
of Denmylne), a birdcage belfry, a porch and
three buttresses. It was repaired in 1803,
abandoned 1827, and in 1856 underwent
restoration which confused the original
architecture and introduced lapped skews and
gableted skewputts. Now a roofless shell. The
gate has 17th century roll-moulded jambs and is
flanked on the north by **Offertory House**, 1748,
and on south by small **Gig House** with quaint
forestair to loft.

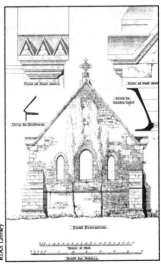

Abdie House (former manse),
1840, Thomas Brown
A change from the conventional Georgian, being
asymmetric with Tudor hood-moulds and
Jacobean gables. Matching porch, 1878.

REFERENCES

ADAMS, I H, **The Making of Urban Scotland**, 1978; BILLINGS, R W, **Baronial and Ecclesiastical Antiquities of Scotland**, 1845-52; DEFOE, D, **A Tour through the Whole Island of Great Britain**, 1724-6; DUNBAR, J G, **The Architecture of Scotland**, 1978; FENTON, A & WALKER, B, **The Rural Architecture of Scotland**, 1981; FENWICK, H, **View of the Lowlands**; HAY, G, **The Architecture of Scottish Post-Reformation Churches** 1560-1843, 1957; HUME, J R, **The Industrial Archaeology of Scotland; The Lowlands & Borders**, 1976; LINDSAY, M, **The Lowlands of Scotland: Glasgow and the North**, 1953; MACGIBBON, D & ROSS, T, **The Castellated and Domestic Architecture of Scotland**, 1887-92; MACGIBBON, D & ROSS, T, **The Ecclesiastical Architecture of Scotland**, 1896-7; MCKEAN, C, **The Scottish Thirties**, 1987; MCWILLIAM, C, **Scottish Landscape**, 1975; NAISMITH, R J, **Buildings of the Scottish Countryside**, 1985; NAISMITH, R J, **The Story of Scotland's Towns**, 1989; **Ordnance Gazetteer of Scotland**, ed. F H GROOME, 1884-5; SLEZER, J, **Theatrum Scotia**, 1692; **Statistical Account of Scotland**, ed. SIR JOHN SINCLAIR, 1791-99, Vol X Fife; **Statistical Account of Scotland, (New)**, Counties of Fife & Kinross; 1845; **A Statistical Account of Scotland (The Third)**, Fife, Alexander Smith, 1952; WALKER, B & RITCHIE, G, **Exploring Scotland's Heritage: Fife & Tayside**, 1987.

Fife
BARBIERI, M, **Description and Historical Gazetteer of Fife**, 1857; GIFFORD, J, **Fife, The Buildings of Scotland**, 1988; **Inventory of Monuments and Constructions of Fife, Kinross and Clackmannan**, RCAHMS, 1933; **The Kingdom: A Descriptive and Historical Hand-book to Fife**, ed. 'Kilrounie' (J R Russell); **The Kingdom of Fife and Kinross-shire**, ed. Theo Lang, 1951; **The Kingdom of Fife in Days Gone By**, ed. W Ballingall, 1986; LAMONT-BROWN, R, **Discovering Fife**, 1988; MACKAY, A J G, **History of Fife and Kinross**, (County History Series), 1890; MILLAR, A H, **Fife, Pictorial and Historical, its People, Burghs, Castles & Mansions**, 1895; SIBBALD, Sir Robert, **The History Ancient & Modern, of the Sheriffdoms of Fife & Kinross**, 1710; SILVER, O, **The Roads of Fife**, 1987; SNODDY, T G, **Afoot in Fife**, 1950; VALENTINE, E S, **Fifeshire**, 1910; WALKER, J R, **Pre-Reformation Churches in Fife**, 1888; WILKIE, J, **History of Fife**, 1924. Details from the List of Buildings of Architectural or Historical importance prepared and held by District Planning Departments.

Books on local areas (a select list)
BEVERIDGE, D, **Between the Ochils and Forth**, 1888; BENNETT, G P, **The Great Road between Forth and Tay**; BENNETT, G P, **Social Conditions Around the Lomonds**, 1775-1872; BENNETT, G P, **The Past at Work**; CANT, R G, **Old St Andrews**, 1945; CANT, R G, **Georgian and Early Victorian St Andrews**, 1946; CANT, R G, **Central and North Fife: its Landscape and Architecture**, 1965; CANT, R G, **The East Neuk of Fife: its Burghs and Countryside**, 1968; CANT, R G, **Historic Crail**, 1976; CHESHER, S, FOSTER, L & HOGBEN, L, **A Short History of the Villages Charlestown, Limekilns & Pattiesmuir**; CUNNINGHAM, A S, **Markinch and its Environs**; DEAN, P & C, **Passage of Time, The Story of the Queensferry Passage and the Village of North Queensferry**; THE FALKLAND SOCIETY, **A Falkland Guide**; FERGUSON, K, **A History of Glenrothes**, 1982; FINDLAY, A M, **Kennoway: its History and Legends**, 1946; FORGAN, J C, **Maistly 'Muchty**; GEDDIE, J, **The Fringes of Fife**; GEDDIE, J, **The Shores of Fife**; HAY FLEMING, D, **Guide to St Andrews**; KIRKCALDY CIVIC SOCIETY, **Kirkcaldy in a Nutshell**, and **Kirkcaldy Walkabouts**; LISTER, D & GILLES, J, **Largo Kirk**; LORIMER, H, **Kellie Castle**; MCWILLIAM, COLIN, **Culross, a Short Guide to the Royal Burgh**; RANKIN, F, **Auld Buckhyne: a Short History of Buckhaven**; REA, A H, **Lindores Abbey**, 1902; ROBERTSON, M, **Old Dunfermline**, 1979; ROWANTREE BODIE, W G , **Some Light on the Past around Glenrothes**, 1968; RUTHERFORD, D W, **St Fillan's Church. Aberdour**; SMART, R N, **St Leonard's College and Deans Court**, 1977; SNODDY, T G, **Afoot in Fife**, 1950; STEVENSON, W, **Kirk and Parish of Auchtertool**; THIRKELL, A, **Auld Anster**; WEBSTER, J M, **Dunfermline Abbey**, 1948; WILKIE, J, **Bygone Fife, from Culross to St Andrews**, 1931; WILKIE, J, **Bygone Fife, North of the Lomonds**, 1938. Guide booklets or leaflets to individual monuments in the care of Historic Buildings & Monuments, published by HMSO and to monuments in the care of the National Trust for Scotland are also available.

Architects:
Architects and Architecture on Tayside, Bruce Walker & W Sinclair Gauldie, 1984; **Building for a New Age; The Architects of Victorian & Edwardian St Andrews**, ed. John Frew; **St Andrews Architects up to 1914**, R G Cant, St Andrews Preservation Trust Annual Reports, 1966, 1967. **David Bryce 1803-1876**, V Fiddes & A Rowan, 1976; **William Burn**, from **Seven Victorian Architects**, David Walker; **Reginald Fairlie**, Patrick Nuttgens; **The Work of Sir Robert Lorimer**, Christopher Husseey, 1931; **Lorimer and the Edinburgh Craft Designers**, Peter Savage, 1980; **Robert Mylne 1733-1811** A E Richardson.

1. Architrave (projecting ornamental frame)
2. Astragal (glazing bar)
3. Barge (gable board)
4. Basement, raised
5. Bullseye, keyblocked (circular window with projecting blocks punctuating frame)
6. Buttress (supporting projection)
7. Caphouse (top chamber)
8. Cartouche (decorative tablet)
9. Cherrycocking (masonry joints filled with small stones)
10. Channelled ashlar (recessed horizontal joints in smooth masonry)
11. Chimneycope, corniced
12. Chimneycope, moulded
13. Close (alley)
14. Cobbles
15. Console (scroll bracket)
16. Corbel (projection support)
17. Crowsteps
18. Cutwater (wedge-shaped end of bridge pier)
19. Doocot, lectern
20. Dormer, canted & piended
21. Dormer, pedimented (qv) wallhead
22. Dormer, piended (see under 'roof')
23. Dormer, swept wallhead
24. Fanlight (glazed panel above door)
25. Finial (crowning ornament)
26. Fly-over stair
27. Forestair, pillared
28. Gable, wallhead
29. Gable, wallhead chimney
30. Gable, Dutch (curved)
31. Gibbs doorway (framed with projecting stonework)
32. Harling
33. Hoist, fishing net
34. Hoodmoulding (projection over opening to divert rainwater)
35. Jettied (overhanging)
36. Lucarne (small dormer on spire)
37. Margin, stone
38. Mercat Cross
39. Marriage Lintel
40. Mullion (vertical division of window)
41. Nave (main body of church)
42. Pavilion (building attached by wing to main building)
43. Pediment (triangular ornamental feature above windows etc)
44. Portico
45. Quoins, rusticated (corner stones with recessed joints)
46. Refuge (recess in bridge parapet)
47. Ridge, crested
48. Roof, flared pyramidal
49. Roof, leanto
50. Roof, ogival (with S-curve pitch generally rising from square plan and meeting at point)
51. Roof, pantiled
52. Roof, piended (formed by intersecting roof slopes)
53. Roof, slated

54. Skew (gable coping)
55. Skewputt, moulded (lowest stone of skew, qv)
56. Skewputt, scroll
57. Stair jamb (projection containing stairway)
58. Stringcourse (horizontal projecting wall moulding)
59. Transept (transverse wing of cruciform church)
60. Transom (horizontal division of window)
61. Voussoir (wedge-shaped stone forming archway)
62. Tympanum (area within pediment qv)
63. Window, bay (projecting full-height from ground level)
64. Window, oriel (corbelled bay qv)
65. Window, sash & case (sliding sashes within case)

INDEX

FIFE

PERTH
419
410
411
NEWBURGH
413
415
414
412
197
196
AUCHTERMUCHTY
198 199
181
195
RIVER EDEN
GATESIDE
STRATHMIGLO
FALKLAND 170
169
NEWTON OF F
WEST LOMOND
168
EAST LOMOND
167
148
LESLIE 166
LOCH LEVEN
147
R. LEVEN
GLENROTHES
KINGLASSIE
LOCHTY BURN
BALLINGRY
ORE
135 LOCH ORE
140
AUCHTERDERRAN
KELTY
141
LOCHGELLY
M90
SALINE
COWDENBEATH
85
36 35
AUCHTERTOOL
39 38
B914
84
37
A823
83
43
A907
A907
80
42 40
OAKLEY CARNOCK
82
81
41
KINCARDINE-ON-FORTH
51
53
DUNFERMLINE
61 63 A907 76 A921
KINGHORN
46 47 48 49
50
57
78
PETTYCUR
COLROSS TORRYBURN
34 33
M90
60 59 A921
32
ABERDOUR
BURNTISLAND
56 55
CHARLESTOWN
DALGETY BAY INCHCOLM
LIMEKILNS
INVERKEITHING
N. QUEENSFERRY

EDINBURGH

0 1 2 3 4 5   10   20 KM

0 1 2 3 4 5   10 MILES

The Kingdom of Fife

ONCE upon a time I was invited to deliver a lecture in the town of St Andrews. It was in the early 1960s, and I was new to Scotland, and living in Cumernauld. Fife was an unknown Kingdom, only briefly glimpsed across the Forth from the southern shore.

What I experienced, however, on that sunny, summer's day ensured that Fife became a favourite place for our family to visit. Eventually it was to become both our home and our place of work. Amongst the Fifers we found a welcoming community.

It is my privilege, therefore, to commend this Guide to you. It describes a varied and beautiful county, rich in its diversity of landscape, coast and buildings. It is an ancient place, and yet a place for today. Glen Pride is to be congratulated on his tracing the story of Fife in the richness of its buildings and environment, and Colin Wishart for his memorable images.

David Cowling

DAVID COWLING
DIRECTOR OF ARCHITECTURAL SERVICES
Fife Regional Council

© *Author: Glen L Pride*
Photographer: Colin Wishart
Series editor: Charles McKean
Series consultant: David Walker
Cover design: Dorothy Steedman
Editorial Consultant: Duncan McAra

Royal Incorporation of Architects in Scotland
ISBN 185158 256 8
First Published 1990

Cover illustrations:
St Andrews (Duncan Cameron, Private Collection)
Anstruther Harbour (J Jack, courtesy of St Andrews Fine Art)

Typesetting and Makeup: Trinity Typesetting, Edinburgh
Printed by Pillans and Wilson Ltd., Edinburgh